W9-BJS-558

contents

Introduction   4

Designs   6

Patterns   48

Martha   48
Fran   52
Bella   55
Jolien   58
Harwood   61
Benita   66
Louisiana   68
Yolanda   71
Jana   74
Firefly   77
Barista   80
Sloppy Joe   82
Tango   84
Beau   89
Lotte   92
Vali   97
Slouchy   100
Sweetheart   102
Malin   106
Griselda   109
Lucille   112

Useful Information   116
Yarn Information   118
Buying Yarns   119
Acknowledgments   120

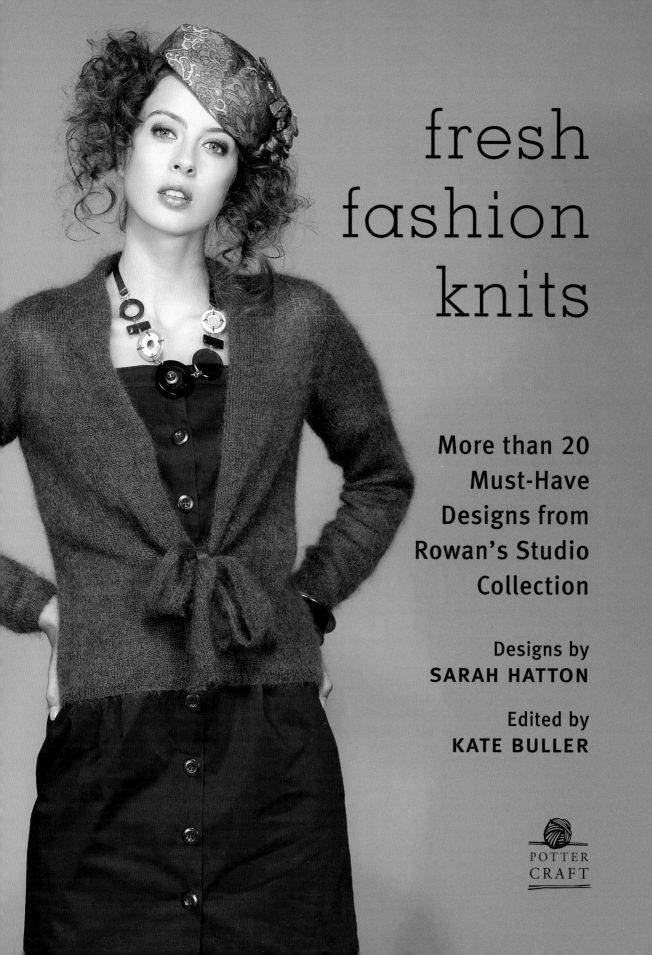

fresh
fashion
knits

**More than 20
Must-Have
Designs from
Rowan's Studio
Collection**

Designs by
SARAH HATTON

Edited by
KATE BULLER

POTTER
CRAFT

Published in the United States by Potter Craft,
an imprint of the Crown Publishing Group, a
division of Random House, Inc., New York.
Originally published in Great Britain as *Rowan
Studio Knits* by Rowan Yarns, in 2010.

www.crownpublishing.com
www.pottercraft.com

POTTER CRAFT and colophon is a registered
trademark of Random House, Inc.

Library of Congress Cataloging-in-Publication
Data is available upon request

ISBN 978-0-307-58661-2

Printed in Singapore

Created and produced by Berry & Bridges Ltd
Suite 416, Belsize Business Centre
258 Belsize Road
London NW6 4BT

Designer Anne Wilson
Editor Katie Hardwicke
Photographer Peter Christian Christensen
Stylist Sarah Hatton
Pattern writer Sue Whiting

10 9 8 7 6 5 4 3 2 1

First American Edition

introduction

Rowan is known to many as a yarn company specializing in beautiful, natural yarns in soft colors and classic, timeless designs. However, knitting's recent growth in popularity amongst the younger generation has only encouraged us to grow our commitment to offer more modern, contemporary designs. The end result of this was to commission our young in-house knitwear designer, Sarah Hatton, to create a series of collections which were produced, photographed, and styled under the Rowan Studio label. Sarah has a great feel for fashion trends straight off the runway, and, most importantly, translates them perfectly into the type of innovative knitwear designs found in this book.

As anyone who knits regularly knows, the nature of a yarn is crucial to the way a knitted garment looks and feels, so the marriage between high quality yarn and great garment shape is an essential part of fashion knitwear design. At Rowan, we spend a lot of time researching new yarns in different weights and natural fibers—merino wool, cashmere, mohair, silk, cotton—with, in some cases, a very small amount of artificial fibers to improve the washability of a yarn, for example. The yarns used in this book include both summer and winter weight yarns, ranging from wools, mohair, and silks to wool and cotton mixtures and pure cottons.

If you are not already a keen knitter, I hope this collection of designs will encourage you to pick up your needles and have a go! To learn to knit is not only the start of a lifelong hobby, but also the opportunity to join an international community of enthusiasts and friends, creating some wonderful, unique, and personal garments for your wardrobe along the way. Visit our website www.knitrowan.com and register today!

Happy knitting!

Kate Buller
Senior Brand Manager
Rowan Yarns

martha

Knitted in a medium-weight tweedy yarn, this vest is great for a casual layered look.

See pattern on page 48.

fran

A great winter cover-up, this cardigan is knitted in a chunky, tweedy yarn.

See pattern on page 52.

bella

Knitted in a mohair-silk
yarn, this little lacy top
looks lovely over a
camisole or a silk blouse.

See pattern on page 55.

jolien

A sporty crop-sleeve top in a soft tweed yarn, this design has a relaxed casual feel.

See pattern on page 58.

harwood

This three-quarter length jacket in a chunky tweed yarn can be dressed up or down to suit the occasion.

See pattern on page 61.

OVERLEAF

benita

Romantically pretty, with its stripy batwing sleeves, this little top is knitted in a fine silk-mohair yarn.

See pattern on page 66.

louisiana

Knitted in a luxurious silk-mohair yarn, this elegant wrap top accommodates all shapes and sizes.

See pattern on page 68.

yolanda

A warm layered jacket
knitted in Aran
tweedy yarn is perfect
for cooler days.

See pattern on page 71.

jana

This cable-pattern
tunic is knitted in a
wool-cotton mix yarn.

See pattern on page 74.

firefly

A pretty wrap top
knitted in a cozy
silk-mohair yarn is just
right for summer nights.

See pattern on page 77.

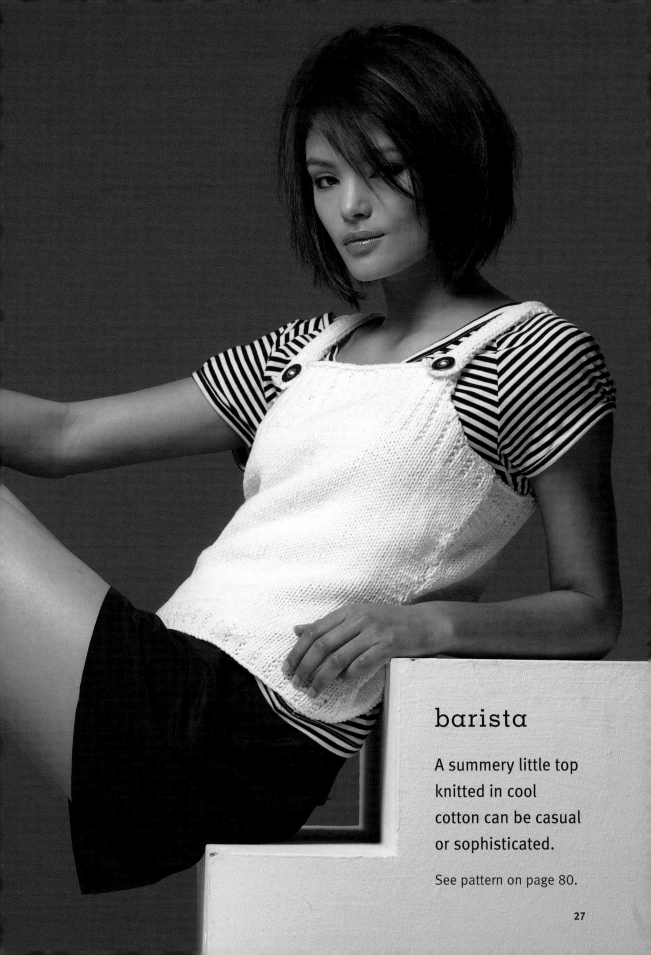

barista

A summery little top
knitted in cool
cotton can be casual
or sophisticated.

See pattern on page 80.

sloppy joe

A warm, soft, cowl-necked top, great for layering, knitted in a thick silk-mohair yarn.

See pattern on page 82.

tango

An elegant flared cardigan, with a pretty stitch pattern, knitted in soft tweedy yarn.

See pattern on page 84.

beau

This sweet cardigan with a tie neck knitted in a silk-mohair yarn, looks equally pretty over a flowery dress.

See pattern on page 89.

lotte

An edge-to-edge jacket
knitted in a cotton mix
yarn with attractive
back detailing.

See pattern on page 92.

vali

This exquisitely soft dress is knitted in a cashmere-wool mix yarn and can be dressed up or down.

See pattern on page 97.

OVERLEAF

slouchy

A great casual top, this one is easy to knit in a fine mohair-silk yarn.

See pattern on page 100.

sweetheart

A classic cardigan with a sweetheart-shaped neckline knitted in fine mohair-silk yarn.

See pattern on page 102.

malin

A sleeveless tunic with a pretty lace stitch pattern, knitted in fine mohair-silk yarn.

See pattern on page 106.

OVERLEAF

griselda

This simple but elegant men's-style top knitted in a wool-cotton mix yarn will go anywhere.

See pattern on page 109.

lucille

This chic short-sleeved cardigan is a great evening cover-up, knitted in a fine mohair-silk yarn.

See pattern on page 112.

martha

See also pictures on pages 6–7.

SIZES

	S	M	L	XL	
To fit bust					
	32–34	[36–38	40–42	44–46]	in.
	81–86	[91–97	102–107	112–117]	cm

YARN

Rowan *Felted Tweed* in Melody 142 (see page 118 for yarn information)

	5	[5	6	7]	balls

NEEDLES

1 pair size 2/3 (3mm) needles
1 pair size 5 (3¾mm) needles
Cable needle

BUTTONS

5 x brass buttons, ½ in. (11mm) in diameter

GAUGE

23 sts and 32 rows to 4 in. (10cm) measured over St st using size 5 (3¾mm) needles, *or size to obtain correct gauge.*

SPECIAL ABBREVIATIONS

C4B = slip next 2 sts onto cable needle and leave at back of work, K2, then K2 from cable needle;
Cr3R = slip next st onto cable needle and leave at back of work, K2, then P1 from cable needle;
Cr3L = slip next 2 sts onto cable needle and leave at front of work, P1, then K2 from cable needle.

BACK

Using size 5 (3¾mm) needles cast on 111 [123: 137: 151] sts.
Row 1 (RS) Purl.
Row 2 Knit.
Row 3 K1, *P1, K1, rep from * to end.
Row 4 P1, *K1, P1, rep from * to end.
These 4 rows form textured patt.
Work in patt for a further 14 rows, ending with RS facing for next row.
Beg with a K row, work in St st, shaping sides by dec 1 st at each end of 7th and 2 foll 16th rows.
105 [117: 131: 145] sts.
Work even until back meas 8¼ [8¾: 9: 9½] in. (21 [22: 23: 24]cm), ending with RS facing for next row.
Work in textured patt as folls:
Row 1 (RS) Purl.
Row 2 Knit.
Row 3 P1, *K1, P1, rep from * to end.
Row 4 K1, *P1, K1, rep from * to end.
Rows 5 and 6 As rows 1 and 2.
Next row (RS) K11 [17: 24: 31], P2, inc in next st, P4, inc once in each of next 2 sts, P4, inc in next st, P2, K51, P2, inc in next st, P4, inc once in each of next 2 sts, P4, inc in next st, P2, K to end.
113 [125: 139: 153] sts.
Work in cable patt as folls:
Row 1 (WS) P11 [17: 24: 31], K2, P2, K4, P4, K4, P2, K2, P51, K2, P2, K4, P4, K4, P2, K2, P to end.
Row 2 K11 [17: 24: 31], P2, K2, P4, C4B, P4, K2, P2, K51, P2, K2, P4, C4B, P4, K2, P2, K to end.
Row 3 As row 1.

Row 4 K11 [17: 24: 31], P2, (Cr3L, P2, Cr3R) twice, P2, K51, P2, (Cr3L, P2, Cr3R) twice, P2, K to end.
Row 5 P11 [17: 24: 31], K3, (P2, K2) 3 times, P2, K3, P51, K3, (P2, K2) 3 times, P2, K3, P to end.
Row 6 K11 [17: 24: 31], P3, Cr3L, Cr3R, P2, Cr3L, Cr3R, P3, K51, P3, Cr3L, Cr3R, P2, Cr3L, Cr3R, P3, K to end.
Row 7 P11 [17: 24: 31], (K4, P4) twice, K4, P51, (K4, P4) twice, K4, P to end.
Row 8 K11 [17: 24: 31], (P4, C4B) twice, P4, K51, (P4, C4B) twice, P4, K to end.
Row 9 As row 7.
Row 10 K11 [17: 24: 31], (P4, K4) twice, P4, K51, (P4, K4) twice, P4, K to end.
Rows 11 and 12 As rows 7 and 8.
Row 13 As row 7.
Row 14 K11 [17: 24: 31], P3, Cr3R, Cr3L, P2, Cr3R, Cr3L, P3, K51, P3, Cr3R, Cr3L, P2, Cr3R, Cr3L, P3, K to end.
Row 15 As row 5.
Row 16 K11 [17: 24: 31], P2, (Cr3R, P2, Cr3L) twice, P2, K51, P2, (Cr3R, P2, Cr3L) twice, P2, K to end.
Rows 17 and 18 As rows 1 and 2.
Row 19 As row 1.
Row 20 K11 [17: 24: 31], P2, K2, P4, K4, P4, K2, P2, K51, P2, K2, P4, K4, P4, K2, P2, K to end.
These 20 rows form cable patt.
Cont in cable patt until back meas 12½ [13: 13½: 13¾] in. (32 [33: 34: 35]cm), ending with RS facing for next row.

Shape armholes
Keeping patt correct, bind off 5 [6: 7: 8] sts at beg of next 2 rows. 103 [113: 125: 137] sts.
Dec 1 st at each end of next 3 [5: 7: 9] rows, then on foll 5 [6: 6: 7] alt rows. 87 [91: 99: 105] sts.
Work even until armhole meas 8 [8¼: 8¾: 9] in. (20 [21: 22: 23]cm), ending with RS facing for next row.

Shape shoulders and back neck
Bind off 6 [7: 8: 9] sts at beg of next 2 rows. 75 [77: 83: 87] sts.
Next row (RS) Bind off 6 [7: 8: 9] sts, patt until there are 11 [11: 12: 13] sts on right needle and turn, leaving rem sts on a holder.
Work each side of neck separately.

Bind off 4 sts at beg of next row.
Bind off rem 7 [7: 8: 9] sts.
With RS facing, rejoin yarn to rem sts, bind off center 41 [41: 43: 43] sts, patt to end.
Complete to match first side, reversing shapings.

LEFT FRONT
Using size 5 (3¾mm) needles cast on 54 [60: 67: 74] sts.
Row 1 (RS) Purl.
Row 2 Knit.
Row 3 *K1, P1, rep from * to last 0 [0: 1: 0] st, K0 [0: 1: 0].
Row 4 P0 [0: 1: 0], *K1, P1, rep from * to end.
These 4 rows form textured patt.
Work in patt for a further 14 rows, ending with RS facing for next row.
Beg with a K row, work in St st, shaping sides by dec 1 st at beg of 7th and 2 foll 16th rows.
51 [57: 64: 71] sts.
Work even until left front meas 8¼ [8¾: 9: 9½] in. (21 [22: 23: 24]cm), ending with RS facing for next row.
Work in textured patt as folls:
Row 1 (RS) Purl.
Row 2 Knit.
Row 3 *P1, K1, rep from * to last 1 [1: 0: 1] st, P1 [1: 0: 1].
Row 4 K1 [1: 0: 1], *P1, K1, rep from * to end.
Rows 5 and 6 As rows 1 and 2.
Next row (RS) K11 [17: 24: 31], P2, inc in next st, P4, inc once in each of next 2 sts, P4, inc in next st, P2, K to end. 55 [61: 68: 75] sts.
Work in cable patt as folls:
Row 1 (WS) P24, K2, P2, K4, P4, K4, P2, K2, P to end.
Row 2 K11 [17: 24: 31], P2, K2, P4, C4B, P4, K2, P2, K to end.
Row 3 As row 1.
Row 4 K11 [17: 24: 31], P2, (Cr3L, P2, Cr3R) twice, P2, K to end.
Row 5 P24, K3, (P2, K2) 3 times, P2, K3, P to end.
Row 6 K11 [17: 24: 31], P3, Cr3L, Cr3R, P2, Cr3L, Cr3R, P3, K to end.

Row 7 P24, (K4, P4) twice, K4, P to end.
Row 8 K11 [17: 24: 31], (P4, C4B) twice, P4, K to end.
Row 9 As row 7.
Row 10 K11 [17: 24: 31], (P4, K4) twice, P4, K to end.
Rows 11 and 12 As rows 7 and 8.
Row 13 As row 7.
Row 14 K11 [17: 24: 31], P3, Cr3R, Cr3L, P2, Cr3R, Cr3L, P3, K to end.
Row 15 As row 5.
Row 16 K11 [17: 24: 31], P2, (Cr3R, P2, Cr3L) twice, P2, K to end.
Rows 17 and 18 As rows 1 and 2.
Row 19 As row 1.
Row 20 K11 [17: 24: 31], P2, K2, P4, K4, P4, K2, P2, K to end.
These 20 rows form cable patt.
Cont in cable patt until left front matches back to beg of armhole shaping, ending with RS facing for next row.

Shape armhole
Keeping patt correct, bind off 5 [6: 7: 8] sts at beg of next row. 50 [55: 61: 67] sts.
Work 1 row.
Dec 1 st at armhole edge of next 3 [5: 7: 9] rows, then on foll 5 [6: 6: 7] alt rows. 42 [44: 48: 51] sts.
Work even until 39 [39: 41: 41] rows less have been worked than on back to beg of shoulder shaping, ending with WS facing for next row.

Shape neck
Keeping patt correct, bind off 9 sts at beg of next row. 33 [35: 39: 42] sts.
Dec 1 st at neck edge of next 5 rows, then on foll 5 [5: 6: 6] alt rows, then on 3 foll 4th rows, then on foll 6th row. 19 [21: 24: 27] sts.
Work 5 rows, ending with RS facing for next row.

Shape shoulder
Bind off 6 [7: 8: 9] sts at beg of next and foll alt row.
Work 1 row.
Bind off rem 7 [7: 8: 9] sts.

RIGHT FRONT
Using size 5 (3¾mm) needles cast on 54 [60: 67: 74] sts.

Row 1 (RS) Purl.
Row 2 Knit.
Row 3 K0 [0: 1: 0], *P1, K1, rep from * to end.
Row 4 *P1, K1, rep from * to last 0 [0: 1: 0] st, P0 [0: 1: 0].
These 4 rows form textured patt.
Work in patt for a further 14 rows, ending with RS facing for next row.
Beg with a K row, work in St st, shaping sides by dec 1 st at end of 7th and 2 foll 16th rows.
51 [57: 64: 71] sts.
Work even until right front meas 8¼ [8¾: 9: 9½] in. (21 [22: 23: 24]cm), ending with RS facing for next row.
Work in textured patt as folls:
Row 1 (RS) Purl.
Row 2 Knit.
Row 3 P1 [1: 0: 1], *K1, P1, rep from * to end.
Row 4 *K1, P1, rep from * to last 1 [1: 0: 1] st, K1 [1: 0: 1].
Rows 5 and 6 As rows 1 and 2.
Next row (RS) K24, P2, inc in next st, P4, inc once in each of next 2 sts, P4, inc in next st, P2, K to end.
55 [61: 68: 75] sts.
Work in cable patt as folls:
Row 1 (WS) P11 [17: 24: 31], K2, P2, K4, P4, K4, P2, K2, P to end.
Row 2 K24, P2, K2, P4, C4B, P4, K2, P2, K to end.
Row 3 As row 1.
Row 4 K24, P2, (Cr3L, P2, Cr3R) twice, P2, K to end.
Row 5 P11 [17: 24: 31], K3, (P2, K2) 3 times, P2, K3, P to end.
Row 6 K24, P3, Cr3L, Cr3R, P2, Cr3L, Cr3R, P3, K to end.
Row 7 P11 [17: 24: 31], (K4, P4) twice, K4, P to end.
Row 8 K24, (P4, C4B) twice, P4, K to end.
Row 9 As row 7.
Row 10 K24, (P4, K4) twice, P4, K to end.
Rows 11 and 12 As rows 7 and 8.
Row 13 As row 7.
Row 14 K24, P3, Cr3R, Cr3L, P2, Cr3R, Cr3L, P3, K to end.
Row 15 As row 5.

Row 16 K24, P2, (Cr3R, P2, Cr3L) twice, P2, K to end.
Rows 17 and 18 As rows 1 and 2.
Row 19 As row 1.
Row 20 K24, P2, K2, P4, K4, P4, K2, P2, K to end.
These 20 rows form cable patt.
Complete to match left front, reversing shapings.

SLEEVES

Using size 2/3 (3mm) needles cast on 79 [83: 87: 91] sts.
Work in textured patt as given for lower edge of back for 14 rows, ending with RS facing for next row. (Sleeve should meas 1¼ in./3cm.)
Change to size 5 (3¾mm) needles.
Shape top
Beg with a K row, work in St st as folls:
Bind off 5 [6: 7: 8] sts at beg of next 2 rows.
69 [71: 73: 75] sts.
Dec 1 st at each end of next 5 rows, then on every foll alt row to 37 sts, then on foll 9 rows, ending with RS facing for next row.
Bind off rem 19 sts.

FINISHING

Press as described on the information page (see page 116).
Join both shoulder seams using back stitch, or mattress stitch if preferred.
Button band
With RS facing and using size 2/3 (3mm) needles, pick up and knit 93 [97: 99: 105] sts evenly down left front opening edge, from neck shaping to cast-on edge.
Beg with row 2, work in textured patt as given for lower edge of back for 8 rows, ending with WS facing for next row.
Bind off knitwise (on WS).
Buttonhole band
With RS facing and using size 2/3 (3mm) needles, pick up and knit 93 [97: 99: 105] sts evenly up right front opening edge, from cast-on edge to neck shaping.
Beg with row 2, work in textured patt as given for lower edge of back for 3 rows, ending with RS

facing for next row.
Row 4 (RS) P54 [55: 57: 60], *yo, P2tog, P12 [13: 13: 14], rep from * once more, yo, P2tog, P9 [10: 10: 11].
Work in textured patt for a further 4 rows, ending with WS facing for next row.
Bind off knitwise (on WS).
Neckband
With RS facing and using size 2/3 (3mm) needles, cast on 8 sts, beg and ending at front opening edges, pick up and knit 48 [48: 50: 50] sts up right side of neck, 49 [49: 51: 51] sts from back, then 48 [48: 50: 50] sts down left side of neck. 153 [153: 159: 159] sts.
Beg with row 2, work in textured patt as given for lower edge of back for 3 rows, ending with RS facing for next row.
Row 4 (RS) P2, P2tog, yo, to last 4 sts, yo, P2tog, P2.
Work in textured patt for a further 4 rows, ending with WS facing for next row.
Bind off knitwise (on WS).
See information page for finishing instructions, setting in sleeves using the set-in method. Attach buttons to correspond with buttonholes, attaching 5th button to inside of right front end of neckband.

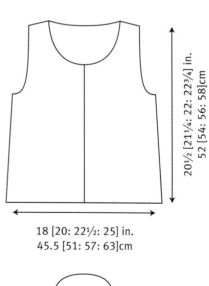

20½ [21¼: 22: 22¾] in.
52 [54: 56: 58]cm

18 [20: 22½: 25] in.
45.5 [51: 57: 63]cm

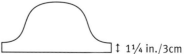

↕ 1¼ in./3cm

fran

See also pictures on pages 8–9.

SIZES

S	M	L	XL	
To fit bust				
32–34	[36–38	40–42	44–46]	in.
81–86	[91–97	102–107	112–117]	cm

YARN

Rowan *Felted Tweed Chunky* in Blue Midnight 282 (see page 118 for yarn information)

16	[18	19	20]	balls

NEEDLES

1 pair size 10 (6mm) needles
1 pair size 10½ (7mm) needles

BUTTONS

3 x gun metal buttons, ¾ in. (19mm) in diameter

GAUGE

11 sts and 20 rows to 4 in. (10cm) measured over patt using size 10½ (7mm) needles, *or size to obtain correct gauge.*

BACK

Using size 10½ (7mm) needles cast on 51 [57: 63: 69] sts.
Row 1 (RS) P1 [0: 3: 2], *K1, P3, rep from * to last 2 [1: 0: 3] sts, K1 [1: 0: 1], P1 [0: 0: 2].
Row 2 K1 [0: 3: 2], *P1, K3, rep from * to last 2 [1: 0: 3] sts, P1 [1: 0: 1], K1 [0: 0: 2].
Row 3 Knit.
Row 4 Purl.

Row 5 P3 [2: 1: 0], *K1, P3, rep from * to last 0 [3: 2: 1] sts, K0 [1: 1: 1], P0 [2: 1: 0].
Row 6 K3 [2: 1: 0], *P1, K3, rep from * to last 0 [3: 2: 1] sts, P0 [1: 1: 1], K0 [2: 1: 0].
Rows 7 and 8 As rows 3 and 4.
These 8 rows form patt.
Cont in patt until back meas 13¾ [14¼: 14½: 15] in. (35 [36: 37: 38]cm), ending with RS facing for next row.

Shape armholes

Keeping patt correct, bind off 3 sts at beg of next 2 rows. 45 [51: 57: 63] sts.
Dec 1 st at each end of next 3 [3: 5: 5] rows, then on foll 1 [3: 2: 4] alt rows.
37 [39: 43: 45] sts.
Work even until armhole meas 8¼ [8¾: 9: 9½] in. (21 [22: 23: 24]cm), ending with RS facing for next row.

Shape shoulders and back neck

Next row (RS) Bind off 4 [4: 5: 5] sts, patt until there are 7 [8: 8: 9] sts on right needle and turn, leaving rem sts on a holder.
Work each side of neck separately.
Bind off 3 sts at beg of next row.
Bind off rem 4 [5: 5: 6] sts.
With RS facing, rejoin yarn to rem sts, bind off center 15 [15: 17: 17] sts, patt to end.
Complete to match first side, reversing shapings.

LEFT FRONT

Using size 10½ (7mm) needles cast on 33 [36: 39: 42] sts.

Row 1 (RS) P1 [0: 3: 2], *K1, P3, rep from * to end.
Row 2 K3, *P1, K3, rep from * to last 2 [1: 0: 3] sts,
P1 [1: 0: 1], K1 [0: 0: 2].
Row 3 Knit.
Row 4 Purl.
Row 5 P3 [2: 1: 0], *K1, P3, rep from * to last 2 sts,
K1, P1.
Row 6 K1, *P1, K3, rep from * to last 0 [3: 2: 1] sts,
P0 [1: 1: 1], K0 [2: 1: 0].
Rows 7 and 8 As rows 3 and 4.
These 8 rows form patt.
Cont in patt until left front matches back to beg of
armhole shaping, ending with RS facing for next
row.
Shape armhole
Keeping patt correct, bind off 3 sts at beg of next
row. 30 [33: 36: 39] sts.
Work 1 row.
Dec 1 st at armhole edge of next 3 [3: 5: 5] rows,
then on foll 1 [3: 2: 4] alt rows. 26 [27: 29: 30] sts.
Work even until 21 [21: 23: 23] rows less have been
worked than on back to beg of shoulder shaping,
ending with WS facing for next row.
Shape neck
Keeping patt correct, bind off 10 sts at beg of next
row. 16 [17: 19: 20] sts.
Dec 1 st at neck edge of next 5 rows, then on foll 3
[3: 4: 4] alt rows. 8 [9: 10: 11] sts.
Work 9 rows, ending with RS facing for next row.
Shape shoulder
Bind off 4 [4: 5: 5] sts at beg of next row.
Work 1 row.
Bind off rem 4 [5: 5: 6] sts.

RIGHT FRONT
Using size 10½ (7mm) needles cast on 33 [36: 39:
42] sts.
Row 1 (RS) P3, *K1, P3, rep from * to last 2 [1: 0: 3]
sts, K1 [1: 0: 1], P1 [0: 0: 2].
Row 2 K1 [0: 3: 2], *P1, K3, rep from * to end.
Row 3 Knit.
Row 4 Purl.
Row 5 P1, *K1, P3, rep from * to last 0 [3: 2: 1] sts,
K0 [1: 1: 1], P0 [2: 1: 0].

Row 6 K3 [2: 1: 0], *P1, K3, rep from * to last 2 sts, P1, K1.

Rows 7 and 8 As rows 3 and 4.

These 8 rows form patt.

Complete to match left front, reversing shapings.

SLEEVES

Using size 10½ (7mm) needles cast on 25 [27: 27: 29] sts.

Row 1 (RS) P0 [1: 1: 2], *K1, P3, rep from * to last 1 [2: 2: 3] sts, K1, P0 [1: 1: 2].

Row 2 K0 [1: 1: 2], *P1, K3, rep from * to last 1 [2: 2: 3] sts, P1, K0 [1: 1: 2].

Row 3 Knit.

Row 4 Purl.

Row 5 P2 [3: 3: 0], *K1, P3, rep from * to last 3 [0: 0: 1] sts, K1 [0: 0: 1], P2 [0: 0: 0].

Row 6 K2 [3: 3: 0], *P1, K3, rep from * to last 3 [0: 0: 1] sts, P1 [0: 0: 1], K2 [0: 0: 0].

Row 7 (Inc in first st) 0 [0: 1: 1] times, K to last 0 [0: 1: 1] st, (inc in last st) 0 [0: 1: 1] times. 25 [27: 29: 31] sts.

Row 8 Purl.

These 8 rows form patt and beg sleeve shaping.

Cont as set, shaping sides by inc 1 st at each end of next [next: 7th: 7th] and every foll 10th row to 39 [39: 45: 47] sts, then on every foll 12th [12th: -: -] row until there are 41 [43: -: -] sts, taking inc sts into patt.

Work even until sleeve meas 18 [18½: 19: 19] in. (46 [47: 48: 48]cm), ending with RS facing for next row.

Shape top

Keeping patt correct, bind off 3 sts at beg of next 2 rows. 35 [37: 39: 41] sts.

Dec 1 st at each end of next and foll 4 alt rows, then on 3 foll 4th rows, then on every foll alt row until 15 sts rem.

Work 1 row, ending with RS facing for next row.

Bind off 3 sts at beg of next 2 rows.

Bind off rem 9 sts.

FINISHING

Press as described on the information page (see page 116).

Join both shoulder seams using back stitch, or mattress stitch if preferred.

Neckband

With RS facing and using size 10 (6mm) needles, beg and ending at front opening edges, pick up and knit 25 [25: 27: 27] sts up right side of neck, 21 [21: 23: 23] sts from back, then 25 [25: 27: 27] sts down left side of neck. 71 [71: 77: 77] sts.

Bind off knitwise (on WS).

Button loops (make 3)

Using size 10 (6mm) needles cast on 18 sts.

Bind off knitwise.

See information page for finishing instructions, setting in sleeves using the set-in method. Using photograph as a guide, sew button loops to right front opening edge and attach buttons to left front so that fronts overlap by 15 sts.

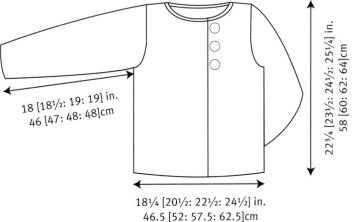

18 [18½: 19: 19] in.
46 [47: 48: 48]cm

22¾ [23½: 24½: 25¼] in.
58 [60: 62: 64]cm

18¼ [20½: 22½: 24½] in.
46.5 [52: 57.5: 62.5]cm

bella

See also pictures on pages 10–11.

SIZES

S	M	L	XL	
To fit bust				
32–34	[36–38	40–42	44–46]	in.
81–86	[91–97	102–107	112–117]	cm

YARN

Rowan *Kidsilk Haze* in Trance 582 (see page 118 for yarn information)

4	[4	4	5]	balls

NEEDLES

1 pair size 3 (3¼mm) needles
1 pair size 5 (3¾mm) needles

GAUGE

20 sts and 30 rows to 4 in. (10cm) measured over 12 row patt rep (chart, page 56) using size 5 (3¾mm) needles, *or size to obtain correct gauge*.

BACK

Using size 3 (3¼mm) needles cast on 91 [99: 111: 123] sts.
Work in garter st for 4 rows, ending with RS facing for next row.
Change to size 5 (3¾mm) needles.
Beg and ending rows as indicated and repeating the 12 row patt rep throughout, now work in patt from chart (see page 56) as folls:
Work even until back meas 13¾ [14¼: 14½: 15] in. (35 [36: 37: 38]cm), ending with RS facing for next row.

Shape armholes

Keeping patt correct, bind off 3 [4: 5: 6] sts at beg of next 2 rows. 85 [91: 101: 111] sts.**
Dec 1 st at each end of next 5 [5: 7: 9] rows, then on foll 3 [4: 4: 4] alt rows.
69 [73: 79: 85] sts.
Work even until armhole meas 7½ [8: 8¼: 8¾] in. (19 [20: 21: 22]cm), ending with RS facing for next row.

Shape shoulders and back neck

Bind off 4 [5: 6: 7] sts at beg of next 2 rows.
61 [63: 67: 71] sts.
Next row (RS) Bind off 4 [5: 6: 7] sts, patt until there are 9 [9: 9: 10] sts on right needle and turn, leaving rem sts on a holder.
Work each side of neck separately.
Bind off 4 sts at beg of next row.
Bind off rem 5 [5: 5: 6] sts.
With RS facing, rejoin yarn to rem sts, bind off center 35 [35: 37: 37] sts, patt to end.
Complete to match first side, reversing shapings.

FRONT

Work as given for back to **.
Dec 1 st at each end of next 5 [5: 7: 8] rows, then on foll 1 [1: 0: 0] alt row. 73 [79: 87: 95] sts.
Work 1 [1: 1: 0] row, ending with RS facing for next row.

Shape neck

Next row (RS) K2tog, patt 34 [37: 41: 45] sts and turn, leaving rem sts on a holder.
Work each side of neck separately.

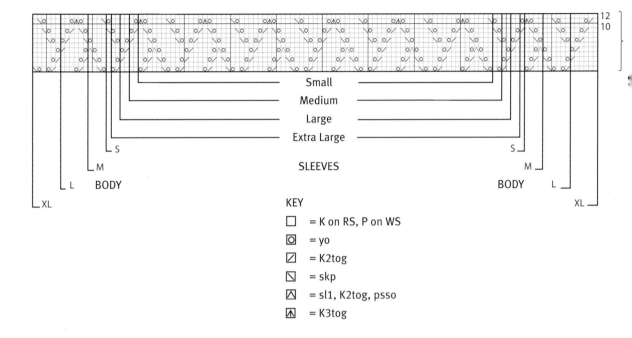

Small

Medium

Large

Extra Large

S

M

L   BODY

XL

SLEEVES

BODY   S

M

L

XL

KEY

□ = K on RS, P on WS

⊙ = yo

⊘ = K2tog

⊠ = skp

⊼ = sl1, K2tog, psso

⊼ = K3tog

Keeping patt correct, dec 1 [1: 0: 0] st at neck edge of next row. 34 [37: 42: 46] sts.

Dec 1 st at each end of next and foll 0 [1: 2: 3] alt rows. 32 [33: 36: 38] sts.

Dec 1 st at neck edge only on next [2nd: 2nd: 2nd] and foll 1 [0: 0: 0] rows, then on foll 17 [17: 18: 17] alt rows. 13 [15: 17: 20] sts.

Work even until front matches back to beg of shoulder shaping, ending with RS facing for next row.

Shape shoulder

Bind off 4 [5: 6: 7] sts at beg of next and foll alt row.

Work 1 row.

Bind off rem 5 [5: 5: 6] sts.

With RS facing, slip center st onto a holder, rejoin yarn to rem sts, patt to last 2 sts, K2tog.

Complete to match first side, reversing shapings.

SLEEVES

Using size 3 (3¼mm) needles cast on 57 [59: 61: 61] sts.

Work in garter st for 3 rows, ending with WS facing for next row.

Row 4 (WS) K3 [2: 0: 2], (K1, M1, K3 [3: 3: 2], M1, K1) 10 [11: 12: 14] times, K4 [2: 1: 3].

77 [81: 85: 89] sts.

Change to size 5 (3¾mm) needles.

Beg and ending rows as indicated and repeating the 12 row patt rep throughout, now work in patt from chart (above) as folls:

Work even until sleeve meas 8¼ [8¾: 9: 9] in. (21 [22: 23: 23]cm), ending with RS facing for next row.

Shape top

Keeping patt correct, bind off 3 [4: 5: 6] sts at beg of next 2 rows.

71 [73: 75: 77] sts.

Dec 1 st at each end of next 5 rows, then on every foll alt row until 41 sts rem, then on foll 7 rows, ending with RS facing for next row. 27 sts.

Bind off 6 sts at beg of next 2 rows.

Bind off rem 15 sts.

FINISHING

Press as described on the information page (see page 116).

Join right shoulder seam using back stitch, or mattress stitch if preferred.

Neckband

With RS facing and using size 3 (3¼mm) needles, pick up and knit 48 [50: 54: 56] sts down left side of neck, K st on holder at base of V and mark this st with a colored thread, pick up and knit 48 [50: 54: 56] sts up right side of neck, then 43 [43: 45: 45] sts from back.

140 [144: 154: 158] sts.

Row 1 (WS) Knit.

Row 2 K to within 1 st of marked st, sl 1, K2tog (marked st is first of these 2 sts), psso, K to end. Rep last 2 rows once more, ending with WS facing for next row.

Bind off rem 136 [140: 150: 154] sts knitwise (on WS).

See information page for finishing instructions, setting in sleeves using the set-in method.

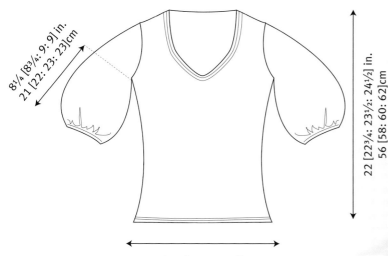

8¼ [8¾: 9: 9] in.
21 [22: 23: 23]cm

22 [22¾: 23½: 24½] in.
56 [58: 60: 62]cm

18 [19½: 22: 24¼] in.
45.5 [49.5: 55.5: 61.5]cm

jolien

See also pictures on pages 12–13.

SIZES

	S	M	L	
To fit bust				
	32–34	[36–38	40–42]	in.
	81–86	[91–97	102–107]	cm

YARN

Rowan *Felted Tweed* in Carbon 159 (see page 118 for yarn information)

	5	[6	7]	balls

NEEDLES

1 pair size 5 (3¾mm) needles

GAUGE

23 sts and 32 rows to 4 in. (10cm) measured over St st using size 5 (3¾mm) needles, *or size to obtain correct gauge.*

BACK

Using size 5 (3¾mm) needles cast on 102 [112: 126] sts.
Row 1 (RS) P0 [1: 0], *K2, P2, rep from * to last 2 [3: 2] sts, K2, P0 [1: 0].
Row 2 K0 [1: 0], *P2, K2, rep from * to last 2 [3: 2] sts, P2, K0 [1: 0].
These 2 rows form rib.
Work in rib for a further 30 rows, ending with RS facing for next row.
Beg with a K row, work in St st until back meas 8 [8¼: 8¾] in. (20 [21: 22]cm), ending with RS facing for next row.

Shape for sleeves
Inc 1 st at each end of next and 3 foll 4th rows, then on foll 5 alt rows, then on foll 11 rows, ending with RS facing for next row. 142 [152: 166] sts.
Cast on 5 sts at beg of next 4 rows, then 9 [11: 13] sts at beg of foll 2 rows.
180 [194: 212] sts.
Work even until work meas 7 [7½: 8] in. (18 [19: 20]cm) from last set of cast-on sts, ending with RS facing for next row.
Shape over arm and shoulders
Bind off 10 [11: 12] sts at beg of next 14 [14: 12] rows, then - [-: 13] sts at beg of foll - [-: 2] rows.
Break yarn and leave rem 40 [40: 42] sts on a holder.

FRONT

Using size 5 (3¾mm) needles cast on 102 [112: 126] sts.
Work in rib as given for back for 32 rows, ending with RS facing for next row.
Next row (RS) K42 [47: 54], (P2, K2) 4 times, P2, K to end.
Next row P42 [47: 54], (K2, P2) 4 times, K2, P to end.
These 2 rows set the sts—center 18 sts still in rib with all other sts now in St st.
Cont as now set until front meas 8 [8¼: 8¾] in. (20 [21: 22]cm), ending with RS facing for next row.
Shape for sleeves
Keeping sts correct, inc 1 st at each end of next and 3 foll 4th rows, then on foll 5 alt rows, then on foll

11 rows, ending with RS facing for next row.
142 [152: 166] sts.
Cast on 5 sts at beg of next 4 rows, then 9 [11: 13] sts at beg of foll 2 rows.
180 [194: 212] sts.
Work even until work meas 2 [2¼: 2¾] in. (5 [6: 7]cm) from last set of cast-on sts, ending with RS facing for next row.

Divide for front opening

Next row (RS) Patt 90 [97: 106] sts and turn, leaving rem sts on a holder.
Work each side of neck separately.
Next row (WS) K1, patt to end.
Next row Patt to last st, K1.
These 2 rows set the sts—front opening edge st now worked as a K st on every row with all other sts still in patt.
Work even until front matches back to beg of over arm and shoulder shaping, ending with RS facing for next row.

Shape over arm and shoulder

Bind off 10 [11: 12] sts at beg of next and foll 6 [6: 5] alt rows, then - [-: 13] sts at beg of foll - [-: 1] alt row.
Work 1 row, ending with RS facing for next row.
Break yarn and leave rem 20 [20: 21] sts on a holder.
With RS facing, rejoin yarn to rem sts, patt to end.
Next row (WS) Patt to last st, K1.
Next row K1, patt to end.
These 2 rows set the sts—front opening edge st now worked as a K st on every row with all other sts still in patt.
Complete to match first side, reversing shapings.

FINISHING

Press as described on the information page (see page 116).
Join both over arm and shoulder seams using back stitch, or mattress stitch if preferred.

Collar

With RS facing and using size 5 (3¾mm) needles, patt across 20 [20: 21] sts on right front holder, patt across 40 [40: 42] sts on back holder, then patt across 20 [20: 21] sts on left front holder.
80 [80: 84] sts.
Keeping patt correct as set, work 1 row, ending with RS of body facing for next row.
Row 2 (RS of body) Rib 9, K4, M1, (K2, M1) to last 13 sts, K4, rib 9.
108 [108: 114] sts.
Work 1 row.
Row 4 Rib 9, K9, M1, (K18 [18: 11], M1) 1 [1: 2] times, K13 [13: 12], P2, K3 and turn, leaving rem sts on a holder.
Work each side of collar separately.
Row 5 K1, P2, K2, P to last 9 sts, rib 9.
56 [56: 60] sts.
Row 6 Rib 9, K to last 5 sts, P2, K3.
Rep last 2 rows until collar meas 6¾ in. (17cm) from dividing row, ending with RS of body facing for next row.
Next row (RS of body) Cast on 33 [37: 41] sts, *P2, K2, rep from * across cast-on sts and to last st, K1.
89 [93: 101] sts.
Next row Cast on 37 [41: 45] sts, *K2, P2, rep from * across cast-on sts and to last 2 sts, K2.
126 [134: 146] sts.
Work in rib as set by last 2 rows for a further 9 rows, ending with WS of body facing for next row.
Bind off in rib.
With RS of body facing, rejoin yarn to rem sts, K3, P2, K13 [13: 12], M1, (K18 [18: 11], M1) 1 [1: 2] times, K9, rib 9. 56 [56: 60] sts.
Next row Rib 9, P to last 5 sts, K2, P2, K1.
Next row K3, P2, K to last 9 sts, rib 9.
Rep last 2 rows until collar meas 6¾ in. (17cm) from dividing row, ending with RS of body facing for next row.
Next row (RS of body) K3, *P2, K2, rep from * to last st, K1.
Next row K1, P2, *K2, P2, rep from * to last st, K1.
Rep last 2 rows 4 times more, then first of these rows again, ending with WS of body facing for next row.
Bind off in rib.

Cuffs (both alike)

With RS facing and using size 5 (3¾mm) needles,

pick up and knit 82 [86: 94] sts evenly along row-end edges of sleeve sections.

Row 1 (WS) P2, *K2, P2, rep from * to end.

Row 2 K2, *P2, K2, rep from * to end.

These 2 rows form rib.

Work in rib for a further 4 rows.

Bind off in rib.

Join row-end edges of cast-on rib strips of right collar. See information page for finishing instructions.

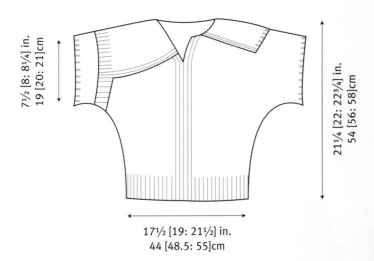

7½ [8: 8¼] in.
19 [20: 21]cm

21¼ [22: 22¾] in.
54 [56: 58]cm

17½ [19: 21½] in.
44 [48.5: 55]cm

harwood

See also pictures on pages 14–15.

SIZES

	S	M	L	XL	
To fit bust					
	32–34	[36–38	40–42	44–46]	in.
	81–86	[91–97	102–107	112–117]	cm

YARN

Rowan *Felted Tweed Chunky* in Sand 280 (see page 118 for yarn information)

	20	[20	22	24]	balls

NEEDLES

1 pair size 11 (8mm) needles
Cable needle

BUTTONS

5 x horn toggles

GAUGE

12 sts and 16 rows to 4 in. (10cm) measured over St st using size 11 (8mm) needles, *or size to obtain correct gauge.*

SPECIAL ABBREVIATIONS

C4B = slip next 2 sts onto cable needle and leave at back of work, K2, then K2 from cable needle;
C4F = slip next 2 sts onto cable needle and leave at front of work, K2, then K2 from cable needle;
Cr3R = slip next st onto cable needle and leave at back of work, K2, then P1 from cable needle;
Cr3L = slip next 2 sts onto cable needle and leave at front of work, P1, then K2 from cable needle;

wyab = with yarn at back (WS) of work.

BACK

Using size 11 (8mm) needles cast on 74 [80: 88: 94] sts.

Row 1 (RS) K0 [1: 1: 0], P0 [2: 2: 2], *K2, P2, rep from * to last 2 [1: 1: 0] sts, K2 [1: 1: 0].

Row 2 P0 [1: 1: 0], K0 [2: 2: 2], *P2, K2, rep from * to last 2 [1: 1: 0] sts, P2 [1: 1: 0].

These 2 rows form rib.

Work in rib for a further 6 rows, ending with RS facing for next row.

Work in patt as folls:

Row 1 (RS) P1 [4: 8: 11], sl 1 wyab, P1, K4, P1, sl 1 wyab, P3, K2, P2, C4B, P2, K2, P3, sl 1 wyab, P1, K4, P1, sl 1 wyab, P4, sl 1 wyab, P1, K4, P1, sl 1 wyab, P3, K2, P2, C4B, P2, K2, P3, sl 1 wyab, P1, K4, P1, sl 1 wyab, P1 [4: 8: 11].

Row 2 K1 [4: 8: 11], P1, K1, P4, K1, P1, K3, P2, K2, P4, K2, P2, K3, P1, K1, P4, K1, P1, K4, K1, P1, K3, P2, K2, P4, K2, P2, K3, P1, K1, P4, K1, P1, K1 [4: 8: 11].

Row 3 P1 [4: 8: 11], sl 1 wyab, P1, C4B, P1, sl 1 wyab, P3, (Cr3L, Cr3R) twice, P3, sl 1 wyab, P1, C4F, P1, sl 1 wyab, P4, sl 1 wyab, P1, C4B, P1, sl 1 wyab, P3, (Cr3L, Cr3R) twice, P3, sl 1 wyab, P1, C4F, P1, sl 1 wyab, P1 [4: 8: 11].

Row 4 K1 [4: 8: 11], P1, K1, P4, K1, P1, K4, P4, K2, P4, K4, P1, K1, P4, K1, P1, K4, P1, K1, P4, K1, P1, K4, P4, K2, P4, K4, P1, K1, P4, K1, P1, K1 [4: 8: 11].

Row 5 P1 [4: 8: 11], sl 1 wyab, P1, K4, P1, sl 1 wyab, P4, C4B, P2, C4B, P4, sl 1 wyab, P1, K4, P1, sl 1 wyab, P4, sl 1 wyab, P1, K4, P1, sl 1 wyab, P4, C4B, P2, C4B, P4, sl 1 wyab, P1, K4, P1, sl 1 wyab, P1 [4: 8: 11].

Row 6 As row 4.

Row 7 P1 [4: 8: 11], sl 1 wyab, P1, C4B, P1, sl 1 wyab, P3, (Cr3R, Cr3L) twice, P3, sl 1 wyab, P1, C4F, P1, sl 1 wyab, P4, sl 1 wyab, P1, C4B, P1, sl 1 wyab, P3, (Cr3R, Cr3L) twice, P3, sl 1 wyab, P1, C4F, P1, sl 1 wyab, P1 [4: 8: 11].

Row 8 As row 2.

These 8 rows form patt.

Cont in patt, dec 1 st at each end of 15th and every foll 24th row until 66 [72: 80: 86] sts rem.

Work even until back meas 23¼ [23½: 24: 24½] in. (59 [60: 61: 62]cm), ending with RS facing for next row.

Shape armholes

Keeping patt correct, bind off 3 sts at beg of next 2 rows. 60 [66: 74: 80] sts.

Dec 1 st at each end of next 1 [3: 5: 7] rows, then on foll 3 alt rows.

52 [54: 58: 60] sts.

Work even until armhole meas 8¼ [8¾: 9: 9½] in. (21 [22: 23: 24]cm), ending with RS facing for next row.

Shape back neck and shoulders

Next row (RS) Bind off 6 [7: 7: 8] sts, patt until there are 10 [10: 11: 11] sts on right needle and turn, leaving rem sts on a holder.

Work each side of neck separately.

Bind off 3 sts at beg of next row.

Bind off rem 7 [7: 8: 8] sts.

With RS facing, rejoin yarn to rem sts, bind off center 20 [20: 22: 22] sts, patt to end.

Complete to match first side, reversing shapings.

POCKET LININGS (make 2)

Using size 11 (8mm) needles cast on 14 sts.

Beg with a P row, work in rev St st for 21 rows, ending with WS facing for next row.

Row 22 (WS) K5, M1, K4, M1, K5. 16 sts.

Break yarn and leave sts on a holder.

LEFT FRONT

Using size 11 (8mm) needles cast on 36 [39: 43: 46] sts.

Row 1 (RS) K0 [1: 1: 0], P0 [2: 2: 2], *K2, P2, rep from * to end.

Row 2 K2, *P2, K2, rep from * to last 2 [1: 1: 0] sts, P2 [1: 1: 0].

These 2 rows form rib.

Work in rib for a further 6 rows, ending with RS facing for next row.

Work in patt as folls:

Row 1 (RS) P1 [4: 8: 11], sl 1 wyab, P1, K4, P1, sl 1 wyab, P3, K2, P2, C4B, P2, K2, P3, sl 1 wyab, P1, K4, P1, sl 1 wyab, P1.

Row 2 K1, P1, K1, P4, K1, P1, K3, P2, K2, P4, K2, P2, K3, P1, K1, P4, K1, P1, K1 [4: 8: 11].

Row 3 P1 [4: 8: 11], sl 1 wyab, P1, C4B, P1, sl 1 wyab, P3, (Cr3L, Cr3R) twice, P3, sl 1 wyab, P1, C4F, P1, sl 1 wyab, P1.

Row 4 K1, P1, K1, P4, K1, P1, K4, P4, K2, P4, K4, P1, K1, P4, K1, P1, K1 [4: 8: 11].

Row 5 P1 [4: 8: 11], sl 1 wyab, P1, K4, P1, sl 1 wyab, P4, C4B, P2, C4B, P4, sl 1 wyab, P1, K4, P1, sl 1 wyab, P1.

Row 6 As row 4.

Row 7 P1 [4: 8: 11], sl 1 wyab, P1, C4B, P1, sl 1 wyab, P3, (Cr3R, Cr3L) twice, P3, sl 1 wyab, P1, C4F, P1, sl 1 wyab, P1.

Row 8 As row 2.

These 8 rows form patt.

Cont in patt, dec 1 st at beg of 15th and foll 24th row.

34 [37: 41: 44] sts.

Work 19 rows, ending with RS facing for next row.

Place pocket

Next row (RS) Patt 8 [11: 15: 18] sts, slip next 16 sts onto a holder and, in their place, patt across 16 sts of first pocket lining, patt to end.

Dec 1 st at beg of 4th and foll 24th row.

32 [35: 39: 42] sts.

Work even until left front matches back to beg of armhole shaping, ending with RS facing for next row.

Shape armhole

Keeping patt correct, bind off 3 sts at beg of next row.

29 [32: 36: 39] sts.

Work 1 row.

Dec 1 st at armhole edge of next 1 [3: 5: 7] rows, then on foll 3 alt rows.

25 [26: 28: 29] sts.

Work even until 13 [13: 15: 15] rows less have been worked than on back to beg of shoulder shaping, ending with WS facing for next row.

Shape neck

Keeping patt correct, bind off 5 sts at beg of next row.

20 [21: 23: 24] sts.

Dec 1 st at neck edge of next 5 rows, then on foll 2 [2: 3: 3] alt rows.

13 [14: 15: 16] sts.

Work 3 rows, ending with RS facing for next row.

Shape shoulder

Bind off 6 [7: 7: 8] sts at beg of next row.

Work 1 row.

Bind off rem 7 [7: 8: 8] sts.

RIGHT FRONT

Using size 11 (8mm) needles cast on 36 [39: 43: 46] sts.

Row 1 (RS) P2, *K2, P2, rep from * to last 2 [1: 1: 0] sts, K2 [1: 1: 0].

Row 2 P0 [1: 1: 0], K0 [2: 2: 2], *P2, K2, rep from * to end.

These 2 rows form rib.

Work in rib for a further 6 rows, ending with RS facing for next row.

Work in patt as folls:

Row 1 (RS) P1, sl 1 wyab, P1, K4, P1, sl 1 wyab, P3, K2, P2, C4B, P2, K2, P3, sl 1 wyab, P1, K4, P1, sl 1 wyab, P1 [4: 8: 11].

Row 2 K1 [4: 8: 11], P1, K1, P4, K1, P1, K3, P2, K2, P4, K2, P2, K3, P1, K1, P4, K1, P1, K1.

Row 3 P1, sl 1 wyab, P1, C4B, P1, sl 1 wyab, P3, (Cr3L, Cr3R) twice, P3, sl 1 wyab, P1, C4F, P1, sl 1 wyab, P1 [4: 8: 11].

Row 4 K1 [4: 8: 11], P1, K1, P4, K1, P1, K4, P4, K2,

P4, K4, P1, K1, P4, K1, P1, K1.

Row 5 P1, sl 1 wyab, P1, K4, P1, sl 1 wyab, P4, C4B, P2, C4B, P4, sl 1 wyab, P1, K4, P1, sl 1 wyab, P1 [4: 8: 11].

Row 6 As row 4.

Row 7 P1, sl 1 wyab, P1, C4B, P1, sl 1 wyab, P3, (Cr3R, Cr3L) twice, P3, sl 1 wyab, P1, C4F, P1, sl 1 wyab, P1 [4: 8: 11].

Row 8 As row 2.

These 8 rows form patt.

Cont in patt, dec 1 st at end of 15th and foll 24th row.

34 [37: 41: 44] sts.

Work 19 rows, ending with RS facing for next row.

Place pocket

Next row (RS) Patt 10 sts, slip next 16 sts onto a holder and, in their place, patt across 16 sts of second pocket lining, patt to end.

Complete to match left front, reversing shapings.

SLEEVES

Using size 11 (8mm) needles cast on 34 [36: 38: 38] sts.

Row 1 (RS) P0 [1: 2: 2], *K2, P2, rep from * to last 2 [3: 0: 0] sts, K2 [2: 0: 0], P0 [1: 0: 0].

Row 2 K0 [1: 2: 2], *P2, K2, rep from * to last 2 [3: 0: 0] sts, P2 [2: 0: 0], K0 [1: 0: 0].

These 2 rows form rib.

Work in rib for a further 6 rows, ending with RS facing for next row.

Work in patt as folls:

Row 1 (RS) P7 [8: 9: 9], sl 1 wyab, P3, K2, P2, C4B, P2, K2, P3, sl 1 wyab, P to end.

Row 2 K7 [8: 9: 9], P1, K3, P2, K2, P4, K2, P2, K3, P1, K to end.

Row 3 P7 [8: 9: 9], sl 1 wyab, P3, (Cr3L, Cr3R) twice, P3, sl 1 wyab, P to end.

Row 4 K7 [8: 9: 9], P1, K4, P4, K2, P4, K4, P1, K to end.

Row 5 P7 [8: 9: 9], sl 1 wyab, P4, C4B, P2, C4F, P4, sl 1 wyab, P to end.

Row 6 As row 4.

Row 7 P7 [8: 9: 9], sl 1 wyab, P3, (Cr3R, Cr3L) twice, P3, sl 1 wyab, P to end.

Row 8 As row 2.

These 8 rows form patt.

Cont in patt, shaping sides by inc 1 st at each end of next [next: 3rd: next] and every foll 8th [10th: 10th: 8th] row to 38 [48: 50: 48] sts, then on every foll 10th [-: -: 10th] row until there are 46 [-: -: 52] sts, taking inc sts into rev St st.

Work even until sleeve meas 17¾ [18: 18½: 18½] in. (45 [46: 47: 47]cm), ending with RS facing for next row.

Shape top

Keeping patt correct, bind off 3 sts at beg of next 2 rows.

40 [42: 44: 46] sts.

Dec 1 st at each end of next 3 rows, then on every foll alt row to 26 sts, then on foll 7 rows, ending with RS facing for next row.

Bind off rem 12 sts.

FINISHING

Press as described on the information page (see page 116).

Join both shoulder seams using back stitch, or mattress stitch if preferred.

Collar

With RS facing and using size 11 (8mm) needles, beg and ending at front opening edges, pick up and knit 17 [17: 19: 19] sts up right side of neck, 22 [22: 24: 24] sts from back, then 17 [17: 19: 19] sts down left side of neck.

56 [56: 62: 62] sts.

Next row (WS of body, RS of collar) K1 [1: 3: 3], inc in next st, (K3 [3: 4: 4], inc in next st) 13 [13: 11: 11] times, K to end.

70 [70: 74: 74] sts.

Work in patt as folls:

Row 1 (RS) K2, P4, *K2, P2, rep from * to last 8 sts, K2, P4, K2.

Row 2 P2, C4B, *P2, K2, rep from * to last 8 sts, P2, C4F, P2.

Row 3 As row 1.

Row 4 P2, K4, *P2, K2, rep from * to last 8 sts, P2, K4, P2.

These 4 rows form patt.

Cont in patt until collar meas 6 in. (15cm) from pick-up row, ending with RS of collar facing for next row.

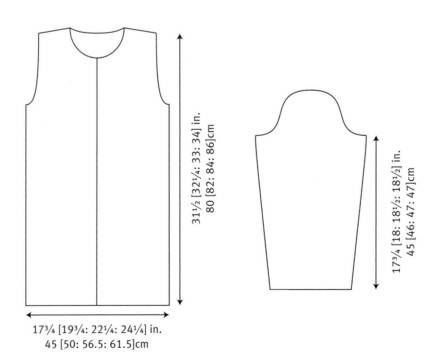

31½ [32¼: 33: 34] in.
80 [82: 84: 86]cm

17¾ [19¾: 22¼: 24¼] in.
45 [50: 56.5: 61.5]cm

17¾ [18: 18½: 18½] in.
45 [46: 47: 47]cm

Bind off in patt.

Button band

With RS facing and using size 11 (8mm) needles, cast on 20 sts, beg at collar pick-up row, pick up and knit 96 [96: 100: 100] sts evenly down left front opening edge to cast-on edge.

116 [116: 120: 120] sts.

Row 1 (WS) K1, P2, *K2, P2, rep from * to last st, K1.

Row 2 K3, *P2, K2, rep from * to last st, K1.

These 2 rows form rib.

Work in rib for a further 5 rows, ending with RS facing for next row.

Bind off in rib.

Buttonhole band

With RS facing and using size 11 (8mm) needles, beg at cast-on edge, pick up and knit 96 [96: 100: 100] sts evenly up right front opening edge to collar pick-up row, turn and cast on 20 sts.

116 [116: 120: 120] sts.

Work in rib as given for button band for 2 rows, ending with WS facing for next row.

Row 3 (WS) Rib 22, *work 2 tog, yo (to make a buttonhole), rib 15 [15: 16: 16], rep from * 3 times more, work 2 tog, yo (to make 5th buttonhole), rib to end.

Work in rib for a further 4 rows, ending with RS facing for next row.

Bind off in rib.

Slip st cast-on edges of bands to row-end edges of collar.

Pocket tops (both alike)

Slip 16 sts from pocket holder onto size 11 (8mm) needles and rejoin yarn with RS facing.

Beg with row 2, work in rib as given for button band for 5 rows, ending with WS facing for next row.

Bind off in rib (on WS).

See information page for finishing instructions, setting in sleeves using the set-in method.

benita

See also pictures on pages 16–17.

SIZES

	S	M	L	XL	
To fit bust					
	32–34	[36–38	40–42	44–46]	in.
	81–86	[91–97	102–107	112–117]	cm

YARN

Rowan *Kidsilk Haze* (see page 118 for yarn information)

A Cream 634

	6	[6	7	7]	balls

B Wicked 599

	2	[2	2	2]	balls

NEEDLES

1 pair size 8 (5mm) needles
1 pair size 9 (5½mm) needles

GAUGE

16 sts and 29 rows to 4 in. (10cm) measured over garter st, 18 sts and 21 rows to 4 in. (10cm) measured over St st, both using size 9 (5½mm) needles, *or size to obtain correct gauge,* and yarn doubled.

BACK

Using size 8 (5mm) needles and yarn A doubled cast on 82 [90: 102: 110] sts.
Row 1 (RS) K2, *P2, K2, rep from * to end.
Row 2 P2, *K2, P2, rep from * to end.
These 2 rows form rib.
Work in rib for a further 4 rows, inc 0 [1: 0: 1] st at each end of last row and ending with RS facing for next row.
82 [92: 102: 112] sts.
Change to size 9 (5½mm) needles.
Beg with a K row, work in St st, inc 1 st at each end of 7th and every foll 12th row until there are 88 [98: 108: 118] sts.
Work even until back meas 21¼ [22: 22¾: 23½] in. (54 [56: 58: 60]cm), ending with RS facing for next row.
Shape shoulders and back neck
Next row (RS) Bind off 12 [14: 16: 19] sts, K until there are 15 [18: 20: 22] sts on right needle and turn, leaving rem sts on a holder.
Work each side of neck separately.
Bind off 3 sts at beg of next row.
Bind off rem 12 [15: 17: 19] sts.
With RS facing, rejoin yarn to rem sts, bind off center 34 [34: 36: 36] sts, K to end.
Complete to match first side, reversing shapings.

FRONT

Work as given for back until 18 [18: 20: 20] rows less have been worked than on back to beg of shoulder shaping, ending with RS facing for next row.
Shape neck
Next row (RS) K33 [38: 43: 48] and turn, leaving rem sts on a holder.
Work each side of neck separately.
Dec 1 st at neck edge of next 8 rows, then on foll 1 [1: 2: 2] alt rows.

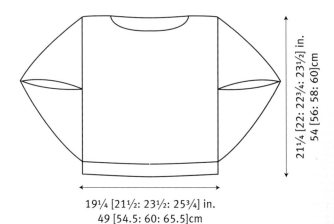

21¼ [22: 22¾: 23½] in.
54 [56: 58: 60]cm

19¼ [21½: 23½: 25¾] in.
49 [54.5: 60: 65.5]cm

24 [29: 33: 38] sts.
Work 7 rows, ending with RS facing for next row.
Shape shoulder
Bind off 12 [14: 16: 19] sts at beg of next row.
Work 1 row.
Bind off rem 12 [15: 17: 19] sts.
With RS facing, rejoin yarn to rem sts, bind off center 22 sts, K to end.
Complete to match first side, reversing shapings.

SIDE PANELS (make 2)
Using size 9 (5½mm) needles and yarn A doubledcast on 87 [90: 93: 96] sts.
Using yarn A doubled, work in garter st for 4 rows.
Join in yarn B doubled.
Using yarn B doubled, work in garter st for 4 rows.
Last 8 rows form striped garter st.
Rep last 8 rows 7 [7: 8: 8] times more, then first 4 of these rows again, ending with RS facing for next row.
Bind off very loosely.

FINISHING
Press as described on the information page (see page 116).
Join right shoulder seam using back stitch, or mattress stitch if preferred.

Neckband
With RS facing, using size 8 (5mm) needles and yarn A doubled, pick up and knit 17 [17: 19: 19] sts down left side of neck, 22 sts from front, 17 [17: 19: 19] sts up right side of neck, then 40 [40: 42: 42] sts from back.
96 [96: 102: 102] sts.
Work in garter st for 4 rows, ending with WS facing for next row.
Bind off knitwise (on WS).
Join left shoulder and neckband seam. Join side seams for first 6 rows from cast-on edge.
Sew bound-off edge of side piece to row-end edge of back between top of side seam and shoulder seam.
Using photograph as a guide, fold in row-end edges of side piece and sew to row-end edge of front, matching ends of cast-on edge of side piece half way up edge.
See information page for finishing instructions.

louisiana

See also pictures on pages 18–19.

SIZES

S	M	L	XL	
To fit bust				
32–34	[36–38	40–42	44–46]	in.
81–86	[91–97	102–107	112–117]	cm

YARN

Rowan *Kidsilk Aura* in Forest 761 (see page 118 for yarn information)

7	[8	9	10]	balls

NEEDLES

1 pair size 6 (4mm) needles
1 pair size 8 (5mm) needles

GAUGE

16 sts and 23 rows to 4 in. (10cm) measured over St st using size 8 (5mm) needles, *or size to obtain correct gauge.*

BACK

Using size 6 (4mm) needles cast on 75 [83: 93: 101] sts.
Row 1 (RS) K1, *P1, K1, rep from * to end.
Row 2 P1, *K1, P1, rep from * to end.
These 2 rows form rib.
Work in rib for a further 2 rows, dec 1 st at end of last row and ending with RS facing for next row.
74 [82: 92: 100] sts.
Change to size 8 (5mm) needles.
Beg with a K row, work in St st until back meas 13 [13½: 13¾: 14¼] in. (33 [34: 35: 36]cm), ending with RS facing for next row.

Shape armholes
Bind off 3 [5: 5: 6] sts at beg of next 2 rows.
68 [72: 82: 88] sts.
Next row (RS) K2, P1, K1, P1, skp, K to last 7 sts, K2tog, P1, K1, P1, K2.
Next row (K1, P1) twice, K1, P2tog, P to last 7 sts, P2tog tbl, K1, (P1, K1) twice.
These 2 rows set the sts—armhole edge 6 sts in rib with center sts in St st—and decreases.
Cont as set, dec 1 st at each end of next 3 [3: 3: 5] rows, then on foll 3 [4: 6: 5] alt rows.
52 [54: 60: 64] sts.
Work 3 [3: 1: 5] rows, ending with RS facing for next row.
Next row (RS) K2, P1, K1, P1, K to last 5 sts, P1, K1, P1, K2.
Next row (K1, P1) 3 times, K to last 6 sts, (P1, K1) 3 times.
These 2 rows set the sts—armhole edge 6 sts still in rib with center sts now in garter st.
Work even until armhole meas 7½ [8: 8¼: 8¾] in. (19 [20: 21: 22]cm), ending with RS facing for next row.

Shape shoulders and back neck
Bind off 4 [4: 5: 5] sts at beg of next 2 rows.
44 [46: 50: 54] sts.
Next row (RS) Bind off 4 [4: 5: 5] sts, patt until there are 7 [8: 8: 10] sts on right needle and turn, leaving rem sts on a holder.
Work each side of neck separately.
Bind off 4 sts at beg of next row.

Bind off rem 3 [4: 4: 6] sts.

With RS facing, rejoin yarn to rem sts, bind off center 22 [22: 24: 24] sts, patt to end.

Complete to match first side, reversing shapings.

LEFT FRONT

Using size 6 (4mm) needles cast on 62 [66: 70: 74] sts.

Row 1 (RS) *K1, P1, rep from * to last 2 sts, K2.

Row 2 *K1, P1, rep from * to end.

These 2 rows form rib.

Work in rib for a further 2 rows, dec 1 [1: 0: 0] st at end of last row and ending with RS facing for next row. 61 [65: 70: 74] sts.

Change to size 8 (5mm) needles.

Row 5 (RS) K to last 5 sts, P1, K1, P1, K2.

Row 6 (K1, P1) twice, K1, P to end.

These 2 rows set the sts—front opening edge 5 sts still in rib with all other sts now in St st.

Cont as set until 24 rows less have been worked than on back to beg of armhole shaping, ending with RS facing for next row.

Shape front slope

Dec 1 st at end of next row and at same edge on foll 18 [16: 16: 12] rows, then on foll 2 [3: 3: 5] alt rows. 40 [45: 50: 56] sts.

Work 1 row, ending with RS facing for next row.

Shape armhole

Bind off 3 [5: 5: 6] sts at beg and dec 1 st at end of next row. 36 [39: 44: 49] sts.

Work 1 row.

Next row (RS) K2, P1, K1, P1, skp, K to last 2 sts, K2tog.

Next row P to last 7 sts, P2tog tbl, K1, (P1, K1) twice.

These 2 rows set the sts—armhole edge 6 sts in rib with front opening edge sts in St st—and decreases.

Cont as set, dec 1 st at armhole edge of next 3 [3: 3: 5] rows, then on foll 3 [4: 6: 5] alt rows and at same time dec 1 st at front slope edge of next and foll 4 [5: 7: 7] alt rows.

22 [23: 24: 28] sts.

Work 3 [3: 1: 5] rows, dec 1 [1: 0: 1] st at front

slope edge of 2nd [2nd: 0: 2nd] and foll 0 [0: 0: 1] alt row and ending with RS facing for next row. 21 [22: 24: 26] sts.

Next row (RS) K2, P1, K1, P1, K to last 2 sts, K2tog.

Next row K to last 6 sts, (P1, K1) 3 times.

These 2 rows set the sts—armhole edge 6 sts still in rib with other sts now in garter st.

Cont as set, dec 1 st at front slope edge of next and foll 4 alt rows, then on 4 foll 4th rows. 11 [12: 14: 16] sts.

Work even until left front matches back to beg of shoulder shaping, ending with RS facing for next row.

Shape shoulder

Bind off 4 [4: 5: 5] sts at beg of next and foll alt row.

Work 1 row.

Bind off rem 3 [4: 4: 6] sts.

RIGHT FRONT

Using size 6 (4mm) needles cast on 62 [66: 70: 74] sts.

Row 1 (RS) K2, *P1, K1, rep from * to end.

Row 2 *P1, K1, rep from * to end.

These 2 rows form rib.

Work in rib for a further 2 rows, dec 1 [1: 0: 0] st at beg of last row and ending with RS facing for next row. 61 [65: 70: 74] sts.

Change to size 8 (5mm) needles.

Row 5 (RS) K2, P1, K1, P1, K to end.

Row 6 P to last 5 sts, (K1, P1) twice, K1.

These 2 rows set the sts—front opening edge 5 sts still in rib with all other sts now in St st.

Cont as set until 24 rows less have been worked than on back to beg of armhole shaping, ending with RS facing for next row.

Shape front slope

Dec 1 st at beg of next row and at same edge on foll 18 [16: 16: 12] rows, then on foll 3 [4: 4: 6] alt rows. 39 [44: 49: 55] sts.

Shape armhole

Bind off 3 [5: 5: 6] sts at beg of next row. 36 [39: 44: 49] sts.

Next row (RS) K2tog, K to last 7 sts, K2tog, P1, K1,

21¼ [22: 23: 23½] in.
54 [56: 58: 60]cm

18¼ [20¼: 22½: 24½] in.
46.5 [51.5: 57.5: 62.5]cm

P1, K2.

Next row K1, (P1, K1) twice, P2tog, P to end.

These 2 rows set the sts—armhole edge 6 sts in rib with front opening edge sts in St st—and decreases.

Cont as set, dec 1 st at armhole edge of next 3 [3: 3: 5] rows, then on foll 3 [4: 6: 5] alt rows and at same time dec 1 st at front slope edge of next and foll 4 [5: 7: 7] alt rows.

22 [23: 24: 28] sts.

Work 3 [3: 1: 5] rows, dec 1 [1: 0: 1] st at front slope edge of 2nd [2nd: 0: 2nd] and foll 0 [0: 0: 1] alt row and ending with RS facing for next row.

21 [22: 24: 26] sts.

Next row (RS) K2tog, K to last 5 sts, P1, K1, P1, K2.

Next row (K1, P1) 3 times, K to end.

These 2 rows set the sts—armhole edge 6 sts still in rib with other sts now in garter st.

Complete to match left front, reversing shapings.

FINISHING

Press as described on the information page (see page 116).

Join both shoulder seams using back stitch, or mattress stitch if preferred.

Neckband

Using size 6 (4mm) needles cast on 7 sts.

Row 1 (RS) K2, *P1, K1, rep from * to last st, K1.

Row 2 K1, *P1, K1, rep from * to end.

These 2 rows form rib.

Beg and ending at beg of front slope shaping, cont in rib until neckband, when slightly stretched, fits up right front slope, across back neck and down left front slope, ending with RS facing for next row.

Bind off in rib.

Slip st neckband in place.

Ties (make 2)

Using size 6 (4mm) needles cast on 9 sts.

Work in rib as given for neckband for 10 in. (25cm) ending with RS facing for next row.

Bind off in rib.

See information page for finishing instructions.

Sew one end of one tie to front opening edge of right front level with beg of front slope shaping, and one end of other tie to left side seam, level with beg of front slope shaping.

yolanda

See also pictures on pages 20–21.

See also pictures on pages 20–21.

SIZES

	S	M	L	XL	
To fit bust					
	32–34	[36–38	40–42	44–46]	in.
	81–86	[91–97	102–107	112–117]	cm

YARN

Rowan *Felted Tweed Aran* in Soot 729 (see page 118 for yarn information)

24	[25	30	32]	balls

NEEDLES

1 pair size 8 (5mm) needles

GAUGE

20 sts and 27 rows to 4 in. (10cm) measured over patt using size 8 (5mm) needles, *or size to obtain correct gauge.*

BACK

Using size 8 (5mm) needles cast on 99 [109: 121: 133] sts.
Row 1 (RS) K0 [0: 2: 0], P0 [1: 1: 1], *K3, P1, rep from * to last 3 [0: 2: 0] sts, K3 [0: 2: 0].
Row 2 K1 [2: 0: 2], P1, *K3, P1, rep from * to last 1 [2: 0: 2] sts, K1 [2: 0: 2].
These 2 rows form patt.
Cont in patt until back meas 16¼ [16½: 17: 17½] in. (41 [42: 43: 44]cm), ending with RS facing for next row.
Shape armholes
Keeping patt correct, bind off 7 [8: 9: 10] sts at beg

of next 2 rows. 85 [93: 103: 113] sts.
Dec 1 st at each end of next 3 [5: 7: 9] rows, then on foll 3 alt rows. 73 [77: 83: 89] sts.
Work 51 [51: 53: 53] rows, ending with RS facing for next row. (Armhole should meas 9 [9½: 10: 10¼] in./23 [24: 25: 26]cm.)
Shape shoulders
Bind off 15 [17: 19: 22] sts at beg of next 2 rows. 43 [43: 45: 45] sts.
Shape for collar
Inc 1 st at each end of 3rd and 7 foll 4th rows, taking inc sts into patt. 59 [59: 61: 61] sts.
Work 17 rows, ending with RS facing for next row.
Dec 1 st at each end of next and 7 foll 4th rows. 43 [43: 45: 45] sts.
Work 3 rows, ending with RS facing for next row.
Shape shoulder yoke overlay
Cast on 16 [18: 20: 23] sts at beg of next 2 rows. 75 [79: 85: 91] sts.
Work 52 [52: 54: 54] rows, ending with RS facing for next row.
Inc 1 st at each end of next and foll 3 alt rows, then on foll 2 [4: 6: 8] rows, taking inc sts into patt and ending with WS facing for next row.
87 [95: 105: 115] sts.
Cast on 7 [8: 9: 10] sts at beg of next 2 rows.
101 [111: 123: 135] sts.
Cont in patt until shoulder yoke overlay meas 6 in. (15cm) from last set of cast-on sts, ending with RS facing for next row.
Bind off in patt.

LEFT FRONT

Using size 8 (5mm) needles cast on 59 [64: 70: 76] sts.

Row 1 (RS) K0 [0: 2: 0], P0 [1: 1: 1], *K3, P1, rep from * to last 3 sts, K3.

Row 2 K1, P1, *K3, P1, rep from * to last 1 [2: 0: 2] sts, K1 [2: 0: 2].

These 2 rows form patt.

Cont in patt until left front matches back to beg of armhole shaping, ending with RS facing for next row.

Shape armhole

Keeping patt correct, bind off 7 [8: 9: 10] sts at beg of next row.

52 [56: 61: 66] sts.

Work 1 row.

Dec 1 st at armhole edge of next 3 [5: 7: 9] rows, then on foll 3 alt rows.

46 [48: 51: 54] sts.

Work 51 [51: 53: 53] rows, ending with RS facing for next row.

Shape shoulder

Bind off 15 [17: 19: 22] sts at beg of next row.

31 [31: 32: 32] sts.

Shape for collar

Inc 1 st at shoulder edge of 4th and 7 foll 4th rows, taking inc sts into patt.

39 [39: 40: 40] sts.

Work 17 rows, ending with RS facing for next row.

Dec 1 st at shoulder edge of next and 7 foll 4th rows.

31 [31: 32: 32] sts.

Work 3 rows, ending with RS facing for next row.

Shape shoulder yoke overlay

Cast on 16 [18: 20: 23] sts at beg of next row.

47 [49: 52: 55] sts.

Work 53 [53: 55: 55] rows, ending with RS facing for next row.

Inc 1 st at armhole edge of next and foll 3 alt rows, then on foll 2 [4: 6: 8] rows, taking inc sts into patt and ending with WS facing for next row.

53 [57: 62: 67] sts.

Work 1 row.

Cast on 7 [8: 9: 10] sts at beg of next row.

60 [65: 71: 77] sts.

Cont in patt until shoulder yoke overlay meas 6 in. (15cm) from last set of cast-on sts, ending with RS facing for next row.

Bind off in patt.

RIGHT FRONT

Using size 8 (5mm) needles cast on 59 [64: 70: 76] sts.

Row 1 (RS) *K3, P1, rep from * to last 3 [0: 2: 0] sts, K3 [0: 2: 0].

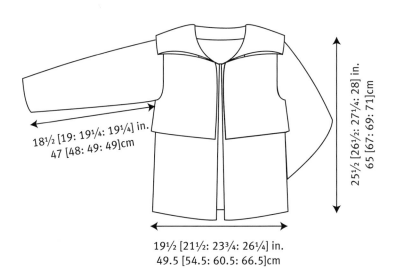

18½ [19: 19¼: 19¼] in.
47 [48: 49: 49]cm

25½ [26½: 27¼: 28] in.
65 [67: 69: 71]cm

19½ [21½: 23¾: 26¼] in.
49.5 [54.5: 60.5: 66.5]cm

Row 2 K1 [2: 0: 2], P1, *K3, P1, rep from * to last st, K1.

These 2 rows form patt.

Complete to match left front, reversing shapings.

SLEEVES

Using size 8 (5mm) needles cast on 47 [49: 51: 53] sts.

Row 1 (RS) K0 [0: 1: 2], P0 [1: 1: 1], *K3, P1, rep from * to last 3 [0: 1: 2] sts, K3 [0: 1: 2].

Row 2 K1 [2: 3: 0], P1, *K3, P1, rep from * to last 1 [2: 3: 0] sts, K1 [2: 3: 0].

These 2 rows form patt.

Cont in patt, shaping sides by inc 1 st at each end of 5th [3rd: 3rd: 3rd] and every foll 8th [6th: 6th: 6th] row to 73 [53: 61: 71] sts, then on every foll 10th [8th: 8th: 8th] row until there are 75 [79: 83: 87] sts, taking inc sts into patt.

Work even until sleeve meas 18½ [19: 19¼: 19¼] in. (47 [48: 49: 49]cm), ending with RS facing for next row.

Shape top

Keeping patt correct, bind off 6 [7: 8: 9] sts at beg of next 2 rows. 63 [65: 67: 69] sts.

Dec 1 st at each end of next 7 rows, then on every foll alt row to 23 sts, then on foll 5 rows, ending with RS facing for next row.

Bind off rem 13 sts.

FINISHING

Press as described on the information page (see page 116).

With WS facing, join both shoulder seams using back stitch, or mattress stitch if preferred, continuing seam up shaped row-end edges of collar and across cast-on shoulder edges of shoulder yoke overlay.

See information page for finishing instructions, setting in sleeves using the set-in method. Join side seams of shoulder yoke overlay. Fold collar in half and slip sleeves through armholes of shoulder yoke overlay sections.

jana

See also pictures on pages 22–23.

SIZES

	S	M	L	XL	
To fit bust					
	32–34	[36–38	40–42	44–46]	in.
	81–86	[91–97	102–107	112–117]	cm

YARN

Rowan *Wool Cotton* in Riviera 930 (see page 118 for yarn information)

	9	[9	10	10]	balls

NEEDLES

1 pair size 3 (3¼mm) needles
1 pair size 6 (4mm) needles
Size 3 (3¼mm) circular needle
Cable needle

GAUGE

22 sts and 30 rows to 4 in. (10cm) measured over St st using size 6 (4mm) needles, *or size to obtain correct gauge.*

SPECIAL ABBREVIATIONS

C4F = slip next 2 sts onto cable needle and leave at front of work, K2, then K2 from cable needle; **C6B** = slip next st onto cable needle and leave at back of work, (K1 tbl, P1) twice, K1 tbl, then P1 from cable needle; **C6F** = slip next 5 sts onto cable needle and leave at front of work, P1, then (K1 tbl, P1) twice, K1 tbl from cable needle; **C11B** = slip next 6 sts onto cable needle and leave at back of work, (K1 tbl, P1) twice, K1 tbl, then (P1, K1 tbl) 3 times from cable needle.

BACK

Using size 6 (4mm) needles cast on 108 [120: 132: 144] sts.
Row 1 (RS) K3, *P2, K2, rep from * to last st, K1.
Row 2 K1, *P2, K2, rep from * to last 3 sts, P2, K1.
These 2 rows form rib.
Work in rib for a further 33 rows, ending with WS facing for next row.
Row 36 (WS) Rib 44 [50: 56: 58], M1,
(rib 10 [10: 10: 7], M1) 2 [2: 2: 4] times, rib to end.
111 [123: 135: 149] sts.
Work in cable patt as folls:
Row 1 (RS) K40 [46: 52: 59], P2, K2, yo, K2tog, P2, (K1 tbl, P1) twice, K1 tbl, P5, K1 tbl, (P1, K1 tbl) twice, P2, K2, yo, K2tog, P2, K to end.
Row 2 P40 [46: 52: 59], K2, P2, yo, P2tog, K2, (P1 tbl, K1) twice, P1 tbl, K5, P1 tbl, (K1, P1 tbl) twice, K2, P2, yo, P2tog, K2, P to end.
Rows 3 to 6 As rows 1 and 2, twice.
Row 7 K40 [46: 52: 59], P2, C4F, P2, (K1 tbl, P1) twice, K1 tbl, P5, K1 tbl, (P1, K1 tbl) twice, P2, C4F, P2, K to end.
Row 8 As row 2.
Row 9 K40 [46: 52: 59], P2, K2, yo, K2tog, P2, C6F, P3, C6B, P2, K2, yo, K2tog, P2, K to end.
Row 10 P40 [46: 52: 59], K2, P2, yo, P2tog, K3, (P1 tbl, K1) twice, P1 tbl, K3, P1 tbl, (K1, P1 tbl) twice, K3, P2, yo, P2tog, K2, P to end.
Row 11 K40 [46: 52: 59], P2, K2, yo, K2tog, P3, C6F, P1, C6B, P3, K2, yo, K2tog, P2, K to end.

Row 12 P40 [46: 52: 59], K2, P2, yo, P2tog, K4, (P1 tbl, K1) 5 times, P1 tbl, K4, P2, yo, P2tog, K2, P to end.

Row 13 K40 [46: 52: 59], P2, K2, yo, K2tog, P4, C11B, P4, K2, yo, K2tog, P2, K to end.

Row 14 As row 12.

Row 15 K40 [46: 52: 59], P2, K2, yo, K2tog, P4, (K1 tbl, P1) 5 times, K1 tbl, P4, K2, yo, K2tog, P2, K to end.

Row 16 As row 12.

Rows 17 to 22 As rows 15 and 16, 3 times.

Row 23 K40 [46: 52: 59], P2, C4F, P4, C11B, P4, C4F, P2, K to end.

Row 24 As row 12.

Row 25 K40 [46: 52: 59], P2, K2, yo, K2tog, P3, C6B, P1, C6F, P3, K2, yo, K2tog, P2, K to end.

Row 26 As row 10.

Row 27 K40 [46: 52: 59], P2, K2, yo, K2tog, P2, C6B, P3, C6F, P2, K2, yo, K2tog, P2, K to end.

Row 28 As row 2.

Rows 29 to 32 As rows 1 and 2, twice.

These 32 rows form patt.

Cont in patt until back meas 19¼ [19¾: 20: 20½] in. (49 [50: 51: 52]cm), ending with RS facing for next row.

Place markers at both ends of last row to denote base of armholes.**

Work even until back meas 8¼ [8¾: 9: 9½] in. (21 [22: 23: 24]cm) from markers, ending with RS facing for next row.

Shape shoulders and back neck

Keeping patt correct, bind off 3 [4: 4: 5] sts at beg of next 4 rows.

99 [107: 119: 129] sts.

Next row (RS) Bind off 3 [4: 5: 6] sts, patt until there are 19 [22: 26: 30] sts on right needle and turn, leaving rem sts on a holder.

Work each side of neck separately.

Dec 1 st at neck edge of next 6 rows and at same time bind off 3 [4: 5: 6] sts at beg of 2nd and 2 foll alt rows, ending with WS facing for next row.

Work 1 row.

Bind off rem 4 [4: 5: 6] sts.

With RS facing, rejoin yarn to rem sts, bind off

center 55 [55: 57: 57] sts, patt to end.

Complete to match first side, reversing shapings.

FRONT

Work as given for back to **.

Divide for neck

Next row (RS) Patt 55 [61: 67: 74] sts and turn, leaving rem sts on a holder.

Work each side of neck separately.

Keeping patt correct, dec 1 st at neck edge of next 10 [8: 6: 4] rows, then on every foll alt row until 22 [28: 33: 40] sts rem.

Work even until front matches back to beg of shoulder shaping, ending with RS facing for next row.

Shape shoulder

Bind off 3 [4: 4: 5] sts at beg of next and foll 5 [5: 1: 1] alt rows, then - [-: 5: 6] sts at beg of foll - [-: 4: 4] alt rows.

Work 1 row.

Bind off rem 4 [4: 5: 6] sts.

With RS facing, rejoin yarn to rem sts, K2tog, patt to end.

Complete to match first side, reversing shapings.

FINISHING

Press as described on the information page (see page 116).

Join right shoulder seam using back stitch, or mattress stitch if preferred.

Neckband

With RS facing and using size 3 (3¼mm) circular needle, pick up and knit 65 [69: 73: 77] sts down left side of front neck, place marker on right needle, pick up and knit 65 [69: 73: 77] sts up right side of front neck, 6 sts down right side of back neck, 48 [48: 52: 52] sts from back, then 6 sts up left side of back neck. 190 [198: 210: 218] sts.

Row 1 (WS) P2, *K2, P2, rep from * to end.

This row sets position of rib.

Keeping rib correct, cont as folls:

Row 2 Rib to within 2 sts of marker, K2tog, slip marker onto right needle, skp, rib to end.

Row 3 Rib to within 1 st of marker, P2 (marker is

between these 2 sts), rib to end.

Rep last 2 rows 6 times more, ending with RS facing for next row.

176 [184: 196: 204] sts.

Bind off in rib, still decreasing either side of marker as before.

Join left shoulder and neckband seam.

Armhole borders (both alike)

With RS facing and using size 3 (3¼mm) needles, pick up and knit 94 [98: 102: 106] sts along row-end edges of back and front between armhole markers.

Row 1 (WS) P2, *K2, P2, rep from * to end.

This row sets position of rib.

Keeping rib correct, dec 1 st at each end of next and 6 foll alt rows.

80 [84: 88: 92] sts.

Work 1 row, ending with RS facing for next row.

Bind off in rib.

See information page for finishing instructions.

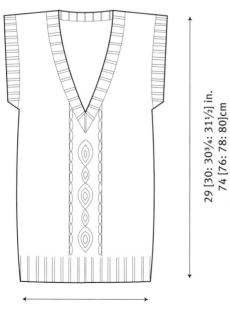

29 [30: 30¾: 31½] in.
74 [76: 78: 80]cm

18¾ [21: 23: 25½] in.
47.5 [53: 58.5: 65]cm

firefly

See also pictures on pages 24–25.

SIZES

S	M	L	XL	
To fit bust				
32–34	[36–38	40–42	44–46]	in.
81–86	[91–97	102–107	112–117]	cm

YARN

Rowan *Kid Classic* in Victoria 852 (see page 118 for yarn information)

7	[7	8	9]	balls

NEEDLES

1 pair size 7 (4½mm) needles
1 pair size 8 (5mm) needles

FASTENINGS

1 decorative kilt pin (optional)

GAUGE

19 sts and 25 rows to 4 in. (10cm) measured over St st using size 8 (5mm) needles, *or size to obtain correct gauge.*

SPECIAL ABBREVIATIONS

MB = (K1, yo, K1, yo, K1) all into next st, turn, P5, turn, skp, K1, K2tog, turn, P3, turn, sl 1, K2tog, psso.

BACK

Using size 7 (4½mm) needles cast on 93 [103: 113: 125] sts.
Row 1 (RS) P0 [0: 0: 1], *K1, MB, K1, P2, rep from

* to last 3 [3: 3: 4] sts, K1, MB, K1, P0 [0: 0: 1].
Row 2 K0 [0: 0: 1], *P3, K2, rep from * to last 3 [3: 3: 4] sts, P3, K0 [0: 0: 1].
Row 3 P0 [0: 0: 1], *K3, P2, rep from * to last 3 [3: 3: 4] sts, K3, P0 [0: 0: 1].
Last 2 rows form rib.
Cont in rib, dec 1 st at each end of 6th and every foll 8th row until 85 [95: 105: 117] sts rem, ending with WS facing for next row.
Row 34 (WS) Rib 10 [10: 12: 14], work 2 tog, (rib 19 [22: 24: 27], work 2 tog) 3 times, rib to end. 81 [91: 101: 113] sts.
Change to size 8 (5mm) needles.
Beg with a K row, work in St st, inc 1 st at each end of 7th and every foll 8th row until there are 89 [99: 109: 121] sts.
Work even until back meas 12½ [13: 13½: 13¾] in. (32 [33: 34: 35]cm), ending with RS facing for next row.
Shape armholes
Bind off 5 [6: 7: 8] sts at beg of next 2 rows. 79 [87: 95: 105] sts.
Dec 1 st at each end of next 3 [5: 7: 9] rows, then on foll 2 [2: 1: 1] alt rows. 69 [73: 79: 85] sts.
Work even until armhole meas 8 [8¼: 8¾: 9] in. (20 [21: 22: 23]cm), ending with RS facing for next row.
Shape back neck and shoulders
Next row (RS) Bind off 8 [9: 10: 11] sts, K until there are 11 [12: 13: 15] sts on right needle and turn, leaving rem sts on a holder.
Work each side of neck separately.
Bind off 3 sts at beg of next row.

Bind off rem 8 [9: 10: 12] sts.

With RS facing, rejoin yarn to rem sts, bind off center 31 [31: 33: 33] sts, K to end.

Complete to match first side, reversing shapings.

LEFT FRONT

Using size 7 (4½mm) needles cast on 39 [44: 49: 55] sts.

Row 1 (RS) P0 [0: 0: 1], *K1, MB, K1, P2, rep from * to last 4 sts, K1, MB, K1, P1.

Row 2 K1, *P3, K2, rep from * to last 3 [3: 3: 4] sts, P3, K0 [0: 0: 1].

Row 3 P0 [0: 0: 1], *K3, P2, rep from * to last 4 sts, K3, P1.

Last 2 rows form rib.

Cont in rib, dec 1 st at beg of 6th and every foll 8th row until 35 [40: 45: 51] sts rem, ending with WS facing for next row.

Row 34 (WS) Rib 6 [7: 8: 10], work 2 tog, rib 19 [22: 24: 27], work 2 tog, rib to end.

33 [38: 43: 49] sts.

Change to size 8 (5mm) needles.

Beg with a K row, work in St st, inc 1 st at beg of 7th and every foll 8th row until there are 37 [42: 47: 53] sts.

Work even until left front matches back to beg of armhole, ending with RS facing for next row.

Shape armhole

Bind off 5 [6: 7: 8] sts at beg of next row.

32 [36: 40: 45] sts.

Work 1 row.

Shape front slope

Dec 1 st at armhole edge of next 3 [5: 7: 9] rows, then on foll 2 [2: 1: 1] alt rows and at same time dec 1 st at front slope edge of next and every foll 4th row. 25 [26: 29: 32] sts.

Dec 1 st at front slope edge only on 2nd [4th: 4th: 2nd] and 8 [6: 7: 6] foll 4th rows, then on 0 [1: 1: 2] foll 6th rows. 16 [18: 20: 23] sts.

Work even until left front matches back to beg of shoulder shaping, ending with RS facing for next row.

Shape shoulder

Bind off 8 [9: 10: 11] sts at beg of next row.

Work 1 row.

Bind off rem 8 [9: 10: 12] sts.

RIGHT FRONT

Using size 7 (4½mm) needles cast on 39 [44: 49: 55] sts.

Row 1 (RS) P1, *K1, MB, K1, P2, rep from * to last 3 [3: 3: 4] sts, K1, MB, K1, P0 [0: 0: 1].

Row 2 K0 [0: 0: 1], *P3, K2, rep from * to last 4 sts, P3, K1.

Row 3 P1, *K3, P2, rep from * to last 3 [3: 3: 4] sts, K3, P0 [0: 0: 1].

Last 2 rows form rib.

Cont in rib, dec 1 st at end of 6th and every foll 8th row until 35 [40: 45: 51] sts rem, ending with WS facing for next row.

Complete to match left front, reversing shapings.

SLEEVES

Using size 7 (4½mm) needles cast on 58 [58: 63: 63] sts.

Row 1 (RS) *K1, MB, K1, P2, rep from * to last 3 sts, K1, MB, K1.

Row 2 *P3, K2, rep from * to last 3 sts, P3.

Row 3 *K3, P2, rep from * to last 3 sts, K3.

Last 2 rows form rib.

Work in rib for a further 11 rows, ending with RS facing for next row.

Change to size 8 (5mm) needles.

Row 15 (RS) K2 [6: 1: 1], inc in next st, (K3 [2: 4: 4], inc in next st) 13 [15: 12: 12] times, K to end.

72 [74: 76: 76] sts.

Beg with a P row, work in St st, dec 1 [1: 1: 0] st at each end of 14th [14th: 14th: -] and every foll 8th [14th: 28th: -] row until 64 [68: 72: 76] sts rem.

Work even until sleeve meas 11½ [12: 12¼: 12¼] in. (29 [30: 31: 31]cm), ending with RS facing for next row.

Shape top

Bind off 5 [6: 7: 8] sts at beg of next 2 rows.

54 [56: 58: 60] sts.

Dec 1 st at each end of next and foll 5 alt rows, then on 2 foll 4th rows, then on every foll alt row until 28 sts rem.

Work 1 row, ending with RS facing for next row.

Bind off 4 sts at beg of next 4 rows.
Bind off rem 12 sts.

FINISHING

Press as described on the information page (see page 116).
Join both shoulder seams using back stitch, or mattress stitch
if preferred.

Collar

Using size 7 (4½mm) needles cast on 273 [283: 293: 303] sts.
Row 1 (RS) K3, *P2, K3, rep from * to end.
Row 2 P3, *K2, P3, rep from * to end.
These 2 rows form rib.
Work in rib for a further 16 rows, ending with RS of collar facing
for next row.
Bind off 74 [76: 78: 80] sts at beg of next 2 rows.
125 [131: 137: 143] sts.
Place markers on sts either side of sts on needle—these
markers match to beg of front slope shaping.
Bind off 4 [5: 5: 5] sts at beg of next 2 [14: 10: 4] rows, then 5
[6: 6: 6] sts at beg of foll 16 [4: 8: 14] rows.
Bind off rem 37 [37: 39: 39] sts in rib.
Sew shaped bound-off edge of collar to front opening and back
neck edges—match row-end edges to cast-on edges of fronts,
markers to beg of front slope shaping, and last set of bound-off
sts to back neck edge.
See information page for finishing instructions, setting in
sleeves using the set-in method.
Fasten fronts using kilt pin as in photograph if desired.

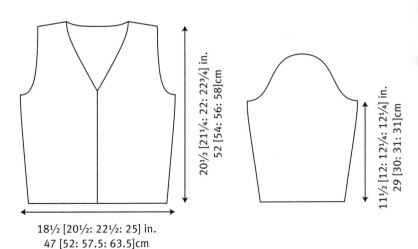

20½ [21¼: 22: 22¾/4] in.
52 [54: 56: 58]cm

11½ [12: 12¼: 12¼] in.
29 [30: 31: 31]cm

18½ [20½: 22½: 25] in.
47 [52: 57.5: 63.5]cm

barista

See also pictures on pages 26–27.

SIZES

6	8	10	12	14	16	
To fit bust						
32	[34	36	38	40	42]	in.
81	[86	91	97	102	107]	cm

YARN

Rowan *All Seasons Cotton* in Bleached 182 (see page 118 for yarn information)

5	[5	5	6	6	6]	balls

NEEDLES

1 pair size 6 (4mm) needles
1 pair size 8 (5mm) needles

BUTTONS

2 x silver buttons, ¾ in. (20mm) in diameter

GAUGE

17 sts and 24 rows to 4 in. (10cm) measured over St st using size 8 (5mm) needles, *or size to obtain correct gauge.*

BACK

Using size 6 (4mm) needles cast on 75 [79: 83: 87: 92: 98] sts.
Row 1 (RS) Knit.
Row 2 P1 [0: 2: 1: 2: 2], *K1, P2, rep from * to last 2 [1: 0: 2: 0: 0] sts, K1 [1: 0: 1: 0: 0], P1 [0: 0: 1: 0: 0].
These 2 rows form textured patt.
Work in textured patt for a further 6 rows, ending with RS facing for next row.
Change to size 8 (5mm) needles.
Beg with a K row, work in St st, shaping side seams by dec 1 st at each end of 3rd and every foll 4th row until 65 [69: 73: 77: 82: 88] sts rem.
Work 11 rows, ending with RS facing for next row.
Inc 1 st at each end of next and every foll 6th row until there are 75 [79: 83: 87: 92: 98] sts.
Work even until back meas 12¼ [12¼: 12¼: 13: 12½: 13½] in. (31 [31: 31: 33: 32: 34]cm), ending with RS facing for next row.
Beg with row 1, work in textured patt for 6 rows, ending with RS facing for next row.
Shape armholes
Keeping patt correct, bind off 7 [8: 8: 9: 9: 10] sts at beg of next 2 rows.
61 [63: 67: 69: 74: 78] sts.
Dec 1 st at each end of next 5 [5: 5: 5: 7: 7] rows, then on foll 1 [1: 2: 2: 1: 2] alt rows.
49 [51: 53: 55: 58: 60] sts.**
Work even until armhole meas 6 [6: 6¼: 6¼: 6¾: 6¾] in. (15 [15: 16: 16: 17: 17]cm), ending with RS facing for next row.
Shape back neck and shoulder straps
Next row (RS) Bind off 3 [4: 5: 6: 6: 7] sts, patt until there are 7 sts on right needle after bind-off and slip these 7 sts onto a holder, bind off center 29 [29: 29: 29: 32: 32] sts, patt until there are 7 sts on right needle after bind-off and slip these 7 sts onto another holder, bind off rem 3 [4: 5: 6: 6: 7] sts.
Using size 6 (4mm) needles and with WS facing, rejoin yarn to one set of 7 sts left on a holder.

Cont in patt on these 7 sts for 8 in. (20cm) for first
shoulder strap, ending with RS facing for next row.
Dec 1 st at each end of next and foll alt row. 3 sts.
Work 1 row, ending with RS facing for next row.
Bind off.
Using size 6 (4mm) needles and with WS facing,
rejoin yarn to other set of 7 sts left on a holder and
work this shoulder strap to match first.

FRONT

Work as given for back to **.
Work even until armhole meas 2¾ [2¾: 3: 3: 3½:
3½] in. (7 [7: 8: 8: 9: 9]cm), ending with RS facing
for next row.
Bind off.

FINISHING

Press as described on the information page (see
page 116).
See information page for finishing instructions.
Using photograph as a guide and adjusting length
as required, lay shaped ends of shoulder straps
onto upper edge of front and secure in place by
attaching a button through strap and front.

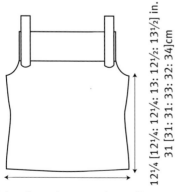

12¼ [12¼: 12¼: 13: 12½: 13½] in.
31 [31: 31: 33: 32: 34]cm

17½ [18¼: 19¼: 20: 21¼: 22¾] in.
44 [46.5: 49: 51: 54: 57.5]cm

sloppy joe

See also pictures on pages 28–29.

SIZES

S	M	L	XL	
To fit bust				
32–34	[36–38	40–42	44–46]	in.
81–86	[91–97	102–107	112–117]	cm

YARN

Rowan *Kidsilk Aura* in Damson 762 (see page 118 for yarn information)

9	[10	11	12]	balls

NEEDLES

1 pair size 8 (5mm) needles

GAUGE

16 sts and 23 rows to 4 in. (10cm) measured over patt using size 8 (5mm) needles, *or size to obtain correct gauge.*

BACK

Using size 8 (5mm) needles cast on 76 [84: 92: 102] sts.

Row 1 (RS) K0 [2: 0: 0], P1 [3: 2: 0], *K4, P3, rep from * to last 5 [2: 6: 4] sts, K4 [2: 4: 4], P1 [0: 2: 0].

Row 2 P0 [2: 0: 0], K1 [3: 2: 0], *P4, K3, rep from * to last 5 [2: 6: 4] sts, P4 [2: 4: 4], K1 [0: 2: 0].

These 2 rows form patt.

Cont in patt until back meas 11 [11½: 12: 12¼] in. (28 [29: 30: 31]cm), ending with RS facing for next row.

Shape for cap sleeves

Keeping patt correct, inc 1 st at each end of next

and 2 foll 4th rows, then on foll 3 alt rows, then on foll 4 rows, ending with WS facing for next row. 96 [104: 112: 122] sts.

Place markers at both ends of last row to denote base of armhole openings.

Next row (WS) K1, patt to last st, K1.

Next row K1, patt to last st, K1.

These 2 rows set the sts—first and last st of every row now worked as a K st and all other sts still in patt.

Cont as now set until armhole meas 8¾ [9: 9½: 10] in. (22 [23: 24: 25]cm), ending with RS facing for next row.

Shape shoulders and back neck

Bind off 11 [12: 13: 15] sts at beg of next 2 rows. 74 [80: 86: 92] sts.

Next row (RS) Bind off 11 [12: 13: 15] sts, patt until there are 14 [16: 17: 18] sts on right needle and turn, leaving rem sts on a holder.

Work each side of neck separately.

Bind off 4 sts at beg of next row.

Bind off rem 10 [12: 13: 14] sts.

With RS facing, rejoin yarn to rem sts, bind off center 24 [24: 26: 26] sts, patt to end.

Complete to match first side, reversing shapings.

FRONT

Work as given for back until 28 [28: 30: 30] rows less have been worked than on back to beg of shoulder shaping, ending with RS facing for next row.

Shape neck

Next row (RS) Patt 42 [46: 50: 55] sts and turn,

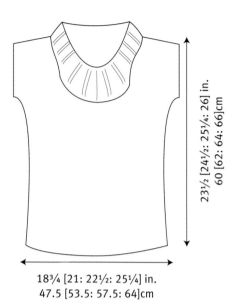

23½ [24½: 25¼: 26] in.
60 [62: 64: 66]cm

18¾ [21: 22½: 25¼] in.
47.5 [53.5: 57.5: 64]cm

leaving rem sts on a holder.

Work each side of neck separately.

Next row (WS) P2, P2tog, patt to end.

Next row Patt to last 4 sts, K2tog, K2.

Working all neck decreases as set by last 2 rows, dec 1 st at neck edge of next 4 rows, then on foll 2 [2: 3: 3] alt rows, then on 2 foll 4th rows. 32 [36: 39: 44] sts.

Keeping sts correct as now set, work 9 rows, ending with RS facing for next row.

Shape shoulder

Bind off 11 [12: 13: 15] sts at beg of next and foll alt row.

Work 1 row.

Bind off rem 10 [12: 13: 14] sts.

With RS facing, rejoin yarn to rem sts, bind off center 12 sts, patt to end.

Next row (WS) Patt to last 4 sts, P2tog tbl, P2.

Next row K2, skp, patt to end.

Working all neck decreases as set by last 2 rows, complete to match first side, reversing shapings.

FINISHING

Press as described on the information page (see page 116).

Join right shoulder seam using back stitch, or mattress stitch if preferred.

Collar

With RS facing and using size 8 (5mm) needles, pick up and knit 29 [29: 30: 30] sts down left side of neck, 17 sts from front, 29 [29: 30: 30] sts up right side of neck, then 37 [37: 40: 40] sts from back. 112 [112: 117: 117] sts.

Row 1 (WS of body, RS of collar) P2, *K3, P2, rep from * to end.

Row 2 K2, *P3, K2, rep from * to end.

Rows 3 and 4 As rows 1 and 2.

Row 5 P2, *K1, inc in next st, K1, P2, rep from * to end. 134 [134: 140: 140] sts.

Row 6 K2, *P4, K2, rep from * to end.

Row 7 P2, *K4, P2, rep from * to end.

Row 8 As row 6.

Row 9 P1, M1, P1, *K4, P1, M1, P1, rep from * to end. 157 [157: 164: 164] sts.

Row 10 K3, *P4, K3, rep from * to end.

Row 11 P3, *K4, P3, rep from * to end.

Rep last 2 rows until collar meas 6¾ in. (17cm) from pick-up row.

Bind off loosely in patt.

See information page for finishing instructions.

tango

See also pictures on pages 30–31.

SIZES

	S	M	L	XL	
To fit bust					
	32–34	[36–38	40–42	44–46]	in.
	81–86	[91–97	102–107	112–117]	cm

YARN

Rowan *Felted Tweed DK* in Scree 165 (see page 118 for yarn information)

	8	[8	9	10]	balls

NEEDLES

1 pair size 3 (3¼mm) needles
1 pair size 6 (4mm) needles
Cable needle

BUTTONS

5 x silver buttons, ½ in. (11mm) in diameter

GAUGE

22 sts and 32 rows to 4 in. (10cm) measured over yoke patt (see page 85) using size 6 (4mm) needles, *or size to obtain correct gauge.*

SPECIAL ABBREVIATIONS

Cr3R = slip next st onto cable needle and leave at back of work, K2, then P1 from cable needle;
Cr3L = slip next 2 sts onto cable needle and leave at front of work, P1, then K2 from cable needle;
Cr5R = slip next 3 sts onto cable needle and leave at back of work, K2, then P1, K2 from cable needle;
C6B = slip next 3 sts onto cable needle and leave at back of work, K3, then K3 from cable needle.

BACK

Using size 6 (4mm) needles cast on 127 [137: 151: 165] sts.
Rows 1 and 2 Purl.
Now work in patt as folls:
Row 1 (RS) P2 [2: 4: 6], (work next 15 sts as row 1 of cable panel, P7 [9: 11: 13]) twice, work next 15 sts as row 1 of cable panel, P5 [7: 9: 11], work next 15 sts as row 1 of cable panel, (P7 [9: 11: 13], work next 15 sts as row 1 of cable panel) twice, P to end.
Row 2 K2 [2: 4: 6], (work next 15 sts as row 2 of cable panel, K7 [9: 11: 13]) twice, work next 15 sts as row 2 of cable panel, K5 [7: 9: 11], work next 15 sts as row 2 of cable panel, (K7 [9: 11: 13], work next 15 sts as row 2 of cable panel) twice, K to end.
These 2 rows set the sts—6 cable panels with rev St st between and at sides.
Cont in patt for a further 22 rows, ending with RS facing for next row.
Place markers on center st of each set of sts in rev St st between cable panels but NOT on center st of row—4 markers.
Row 25 (dec) (RS) *Patt to within 1 st of marked st, P3tog (marked st is center st of these 3 sts), rep from * 3 times more, patt to end.
119 [129: 143: 157] sts.
Now working 5 [7: 9: 11] sts in rev St st between cable panels where decs have been worked, cont in patt as now set for a further 23 rows, ending with RS facing for next row.

Row 49 (RS) As row 25. 111 [121: 135: 149] sts.
Now working 3 [5: 7: 9] sts in rev St st between cables where 2nd set of decs have been worked, cont in patt as now set for a further 23 rows, ending with RS facing for next row. (All 12 rows of cable panels have now been worked 6 times.)
Next row (RS) Purl.
Move markers onto center st of each cable panel—6 markers.
Next row *P to marked st, P2tog (marked st is first of these 2 sts), rep from * 5 times more, P to end. 105 [115: 129: 143] sts.
Now work in **yoke patt** as folls:
Row 1 (RS) K1, *P1, K1, rep from * to end.
Rows 2 and 3 P1, *K1, P1, rep from * to end.
Row 4 As row 1.
These 4 rows form yoke patt.
Cont in yoke patt until back meas 13 [13½: 13¾: 14¼] in. (33 [34: 35: 36]cm), ending with RS facing for next row.
Shape armholes
Keeping patt correct, bind off 6 [7: 8: 9] sts at beg of next 2 rows.
93 [101: 113: 125] sts.
Dec 1 st at each end of next 5 [7: 9: 11] rows, then on foll 2 [2: 3: 3] alt rows.
79 [83: 89: 97] sts.
Work even until armhole meas 8 [8¼: 8¾: 9] in. (20 [21: 22: 23]cm), ending with RS facing for next row.
Shape shoulders and back neck
Next row (RS) Bind off 9 [10: 11: 13] sts, patt until there are 13 [14: 15: 17] sts on right needle and

turn, leaving rem sts on a holder.
Work each side of neck separately.
Bind off 3 sts at beg of next row.
Bind off rem 10 [11: 12: 14] sts.
With RS facing, rejoin yarn to rem sts, bind off center 35 [35: 37: 37] sts, patt to end.
Complete to match first side, reversing shapings.

LEFT FRONT
Using size 6 (4mm) needles cast on 62 [67: 74: 81] sts.
Rows 1 and 2 Purl.
Now work in patt as folls:
Row 1 (RS) P2 [2: 4: 6], (work next 15 sts as row 1 of cable panel, P7 [9: 11: 13]) twice, work next 15 sts as row 1 of cable panel, P to end.
Row 2 K1 [2: 3: 4], (work next 15 sts as row 2 of cable panel, K7 [9: 11: 13]) twice, work next 15 sts as row 2 of cable panel, K to end.
These 2 rows set the sts—3 cable panels with rev St st between and at sides.
Cont in patt for a further 22 rows, ending with RS facing for next row.
Place markers on center st of each set of sts in rev St st between cable panels—2 markers.
Row 25 (dec) (RS) *Patt to within 1 st of marked st, P3tog (marked st is center st of these 3 sts), rep from * once more, patt to end. 58 [63: 70: 77] sts.
Now working 5 [7: 9: 11] sts in rev St st between cable panels where decs have been worked, cont in patt as now set for a further 23 rows, ending with RS facing for next row.
Row 49 (RS) As row 25. 54 [59: 66: 73] sts.

Cable Panel

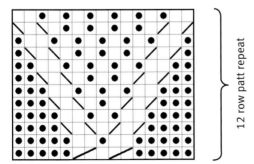

12 row patt repeat

KEY

☐	= K on RS, P on WS
●	= P on RS, K on WS
◢◣	= Cr3R
◥◤	= Cr3L
◿◺	= Cr5R

Now working 3 [5: 7: 9] sts in rev St st between cables where 2nd set of decs have been worked, cont in patt as now set for a further 23 rows, ending with RS facing for next row. (All 12 rows of cable panels have now been worked 6 times.)

Next row (RS) Purl.

Move markers onto center st of each cable panel—3 markers.

Next row *P to marked st, P2tog (marked st is first of these 2 sts), rep from * twice more, P to end.

51 [56: 63: 70] sts.

Now work in yoke patt as folls:

Row 1 (RS) *K1, P1, rep from * to last 1 [0: 1: 0] st, K1 [0: 1: 0].

Row 2 P1 [0: 1: 0], *K1, P1, rep from * to end.

Row 3 *P1, K1, rep from * to last 1 [0: 1: 0] st, P1 [0: 1: 0].

Row 4 K1 [0: 1: 0], *P1, K1, rep from * to end.

These 4 rows form yoke patt.

Cont in yoke patt until left front matches back to beg of armhole shaping, ending with RS facing for next row.

Shape armhole

Keeping patt correct, bind off 6 [7: 8: 9] sts at beg of next row.

45 [49: 55: 61] sts.

Work 1 row.

Dec 1 st at armhole edge of next 5 [7: 9: 11] rows, then on foll 2 [2: 3: 3] alt rows.

38 [40: 43: 47] sts.

Work even until 23 [23: 25: 25] rows less have been worked than on back to beg of shoulder shaping, ending with WS facing for next row.

Shape neck

Keeping patt correct, bind off 9 sts at beg of next row.

29 [31: 34: 38] sts.

Dec 1 st at neck edge of next 7 rows, then on foll 3 [3: 4: 4] alt rows.

19 [21: 23: 27] sts.

Work 9 rows, ending with RS facing for next row.

Shape shoulder

Bind off 9 [10: 11: 13] sts at beg of next row.

Work 1 row.

Bind off rem 10 [11: 12: 14] sts.

RIGHT FRONT

Using size 6 (4mm) needles cast on 62 [67: 74: 81] sts.

Rows 1 and 2 Purl.

Now work in patt as folls:

Row 1 (RS) P1 [2: 3: 4], work next 15 sts as row 1 of cable panel, (P7 [9: 11: 13], work next 15 sts as row 1 of cable panel) twice, P to end.

Row 2 K2 [2: 4: 6], (work next 15 sts as row 2 of cable panel, K7 [9: 11: 13]) twice, work next 15 sts as row 2 of cable panel, K to end.

These 2 rows set the sts—3 cable panels with rev St st between and at sides.

Cont in patt for a further 22 rows, ending with RS facing for next row.

Place markers on center st of each set of sts in rev St st between cable panels—2 markers.

Row 25 (dec) (RS) *Patt to within 1 st of marked st, P3tog (marked st is center st of these 3 sts), rep from * once more, patt to end.

58 [63: 70: 77] sts.

Now working 5 [7: 9: 11] sts in rev St st between cable panels where decs have been worked, cont in patt as now set for a further 23 rows, ending with RS facing for next row.

Row 49 (RS) As row 25.

54 [59: 66: 73] sts.

Now working 3 [5: 7: 9] sts in rev St st between cables where 2nd set of decs have been worked, cont in patt as now set for a further 23 rows, ending with RS facing for next row. (All 12 rows of cable panels have now been worked 6 times.)

Next row (RS) Purl.

Move markers onto center st of each cable panel—3 markers.

Next row *P to marked st, P2tog (marked st is first of these 2 sts), rep from * twice more, P to end.

51 [56: 63: 70] sts.

Now work in yoke patt as folls:

Row 1 (RS) K1 [0: 1: 0], *P1, K1, rep from * to end.

Row 2 *P1, K1, rep from * to last 1 [0: 1: 0] st, P1 [0: 1: 0].

Row 3 P1 [0: 1: 0], *K1, P1, rep from * to end.

Row 4 *K1, P1, rep from * to last 1 [0: 1: 0] st, K1 [0: 1: 0].

These 4 rows form yoke patt.

Complete to match left front, reversing shapings.

SLEEVES

Using size 6 (4mm) needles cast on 69 [71: 73: 75] sts.

Rows 1 and 2 Purl.

Now work in patt as folls:

Row 1 (RS) P4 [5: 6: 7], K6, (P5, K6) 5 times, P to end.

Row 2 K4 [5: 6: 7], P6, (K5, P6) 5 times, K to end.

Rows 3 and 4 As rows 1 and 2.

Row 5 P4 [5: 6: 7], C6B, (P5, C6B) 5 times, P to end.

Row 6 As row 2.

These 6 rows form patt.

Cont in patt, shaping sides by inc 1 st at each end of 9th [7th: 7th: 5th] and every foll 18th [16th: 14th: 12th] row to 83 [87: 87: 85] sts, then on every foll - [-: 16th: 14th] row until there are - [-: 91: 95] sts, taking inc sts into rev St st.

Work even until sleeve meas 18 [18½: 19: 19] in. (46 [47: 48: 48]cm), ending with RS facing for next row.

Shape top

Keeping patt correct, bind off 6 [7: 8: 9] sts at beg of next 2 rows. 71 [73: 75: 77] sts.

Dec 1 st at each end of next 9 rows, then on every foll alt row to 27 sts, then on foll 5 rows, ending with RS facing for next row.

Bind off rem 17 sts.

FINISHING

Press as described on the information page (see page 116).

Join both shoulder seams using back stitch, or mattress stitch if preferred.

Button band

With RS facing and using size 3 (3¼mm) needles, beg at neck shaping, pick up and knit 49 [53: 57: 61] sts evenly down left front opening edge to top of cable panels, then 60 sts down opening edge to cast-on edge.

109 [113: 117: 121] sts.

Row 1 (WS) K1, *P1, K1, rep from * to end.

Rows 2 and 3 P1, *K1, P1, rep from * to end.

Row 4 As row 1.

These 4 rows form patt.

Rep last 4 rows once more, ending with WS facing for next row.

Bind off in patt (on WS).

Buttonhole band

With RS facing and using size 3 (3¼mm) needles, beg at cast-on edge, pick up and knit 60 sts evenly up right front opening edge to top of cable panels,

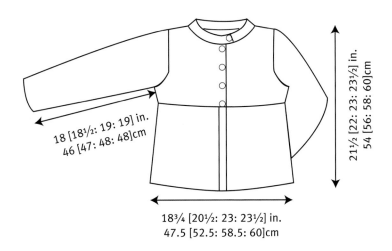

18 [18½: 19: 19] in.
46 [47: 48: 48]cm

21½ [22: 23: 23½] in.
54 [56: 58: 60]cm

18¾ [20½: 23: 23½] in.
47.5 [52.5: 58.5: 60]cm

then 49 [53: 57: 61] sts up opening edge to neck shaping.

109 [113: 117: 121] sts.

Work in patt as given for button band for 3 rows, ending with RS facing for next row.

Row 4 (buttonhole row) (RS) Patt 64 [65: 63: 64] sts, (bind off 2 sts, patt until there are 11 [12: 14: 15] sts on right needle after bind-off) 3 times, bind off 2 sts, patt to end.

Row 5 Patt to end, casting on 2 sts over those bound off on previous row.

Work in patt for a further 3 rows, ending with WS facing for next row.

Bind off in patt (on WS).

Neckband

Using size 3 (3¼mm) needles cast on 8 sts, beg and ending at bound-off edges of front bands and with RS facing, pick up and knit 31 [31: 33: 33] sts up right side of neck, 41 [41: 43: 43] sts from back, then 31 [31: 33: 33] sts down left side of neck.

111 [111: 117: 117] sts.

Work in patt as given for button band for 3 rows, ending with RS facing for next row.

Row 4 (buttonhole row) (RS) Patt 4 sts, bind off 2 sts, patt to end.

Row 5 Patt to end, casting on 2 sts over those bound off on previous row.

Work in patt for a further 3 rows, ending with WS facing for next row.

Bind off in patt (on WS).

See information page for finishing instructions, setting in sleeves using the set-in method.

beau

See also pictures on pages 32–33.

SIZES

6	8	10	12	14	16	

To fit bust

32	[34	36	38	40	42]	in.
81	[86	91	97	102	107]	cm

YARN

Rowan *Kidsilk Haze* in Drab 588 (see page 118 for yarn information)

5	[5	6	6	6	7]	balls

NEEDLES

1 pair size 2 (2¾mm) needles
1 pair size 3 (3¼mm) needles

BUTTONS

4 x shell buttons, ¾ in. (18mm) in diameter

GAUGE

25 sts and 34 rows to 4 in. (10cm) measured over St st using size 3 (3¼mm) needles, *or size to obtain correct gauge.*

BACK

Using size 2 (2¾mm) needles cast on 107 [113: 117: 125: 133: 141] sts.
Row 1 (RS) K1, *P1, K1, rep from * to end.
Row 2 P1, *K1, P1, rep from * to end.
These 2 rows form rib.
Work in rib for a further 6 rows, ending with RS facing for next row.
Change to size 3 (3¼mm) needles.

Beg with a K row, work in St st until back meas 5 [5: 4: 7: 6: 8] cm, ending with RS facing for next row.
Next row (RS) K2, skp, K to last 4 sts, K2tog, K2.
Working all side seam decreases as set by last row, dec 1 st at each end of 10th and 2 foll 10th rows.
99 [105: 109: 117: 125: 133] sts.
Work 17 rows, ending with RS facing for next row.
Next row (RS) K3, M1, K to last 3 sts, M1, K3.
Working all side seam increases as set by last row, inc 1 st at each end of 12th and 2 foll 12th rows.
107 [113: 117: 125: 133: 141] sts.
Work 21 rows, ending with RS facing for next row.
(Back should meas 14¼ [14¼: 13¾: 15: 14½: 15½] in./36 [36: 35: 38: 37: 39]cm.)
Shape armholes
Bind off 4 [5: 5: 6: 6: 7] sts at beg of next 2 rows.
99 [103: 107: 113: 121: 127] sts.
Next row (RS) K2, skp, K to last 4 sts, K2tog, K2.
Next row P2, P2tog, P to last 4 sts, P2tog tbl, P2.
Working all armhole decreases as set by last 2 rows, dec 1 st at each end of next 3 [3: 5: 5: 7: 7] rows, then on foll 3 [4: 3: 4: 4: 5] alt rows.
83 [85: 87: 91: 95: 99] sts.
Work even until armhole meas 7 [7: 7½: 7½: 8: 8] in. (18 [18: 19: 19: 20: 20]cm), ending with RS facing for next row.
Shape shoulders and back neck
Bind off 5 [6: 6: 7: 7: 8] sts at beg of next 2 rows.
73 [73: 75: 77: 81: 83] sts.
Next row (RS) Bind off 5 [6: 6: 7: 7: 8] sts, K until there are 10 [9: 10: 10: 11: 11] sts on right needle and turn, leaving rem sts on a holder.

Work each side of neck separately.

Bind off 4 sts at beg of next row.

Bind off rem 6 [5: 6: 6: 7: 7] sts.

With RS facing, rejoin yarn to rem sts, bind off center 43 [43: 43: 43: 45: 45] sts, K to end.

Complete to match first side, reversing shapings.

LEFT FRONT

Using size 2 (2¾mm) needles cast on 58 [60: 62: 66: 70: 74] sts.

Row 1 (RS) *K1, P1, rep from * to last 2 sts, K2.

Row 2 *K1, P1, rep from * to end.

These 2 rows form rib.

Work in rib for a further 5 rows, ending with WS facing for next row.

Row 8 (WS) Rib 7 and slip these 7 sts onto a holder, M1, rib to last 2 [0: 0: 0: 0: 0] sts, (work 2 tog) 1 [0: 0: 0: 0: 0] times. 51 [54: 56: 60: 64: 68] sts.

Change to size 3 (3¼mm) needles.

Beg with a K row, work in St st until left front meas 2 [2: 1½: 2¾: 2½: 3] in. (5 [5: 4: 7: 6: 8]cm), ending with RS facing for next row.

Working all side seam decreases as set by back, dec 1 st at beg of next and 3 foll 10th rows.

47 [50: 52: 56: 60: 64] sts.

Work 1 row, ending with RS facing for next row.

Shape front slope

Dec 1 st at end of next and 3 [3: 1: 1: 3: 3] foll 4th rows, then on 10 [10: 11: 11: 10: 10] foll 6th rows and at same time, working side seam inc as given for back, inc 1 st at beg of 17th and 3 foll 12th rows. 37 [40: 43: 47: 50: 54] sts.

Work 1 [1: 3: 3: 1: 1] rows, ending with RS facing for next row. (Left front now matches back to beg of armhole shaping.)

Shape armhole

Bind off 4 [5: 5: 6: 6: 7] sts at beg of next row.

33 [35: 38: 41: 44: 47] sts.

Work 1 row.

Working all armhole decreases as set by back, dec 1 st at armhole edge of next 5 [5: 7: 7: 9: 9] rows, then on foll 3 [4: 3: 4: 4: 5] alt rows and at same time dec 1 st at front slope edge of 3rd [3rd: next: next: 3rd: 3rd] and 1 [1: 2: 2: 2: 2] foll 6th rows.

23 [24: 25: 27: 28: 30] sts.

Dec 1 st at front slope edge only on 4th [2nd: 6th: 4th: 4th: 2nd] and 6 foll 6th rows.

16 [17: 18: 20: 21: 23] sts.

Work even until left front matches back to beg of shoulder shaping, ending with RS facing for next row.

Shape shoulder

Bind off 5 [6: 6: 7: 7: 8] sts at beg of next and foll alt row.

Work 1 row.

Bind off rem 6 [5: 6: 6: 7: 7] sts.

RIGHT FRONT

Using size 2 (2¾mm) needles cast on 58 [60: 62: 66: 70: 74] sts.

Row 1 (RS) K2, *P1, K1, rep from * to end.

Row 2 *P1, K1, rep from * to end.

These 2 rows form rib.

Work in rib for a further 2 rows, ending with RS facing for next row.

Row 5 (RS) Rib 2, work 2 tog, yo (to make a buttonhole), rib to end.

Work in rib for a further 2 rows, ending with WS facing for next row.

Row 8 (WS) (Work 2 tog) 1 [0: 0: 0: 0: 0] times, rib to last 7 sts, M1 and turn, leaving rem 7 sts on a holder. 51 [54: 56: 60: 64: 68] sts.

Change to size 3 (3¼mm) needles.

Beg with a K row, work in St st until right front meas 2 [2: 1½: 2¾: 2½: 3] in. (5 [5: 4: 7: 6: 8]cm), ending with RS facing for next row.

Working all side seam decreases as set by back, dec 1 st at end of next and 3 foll 10th rows.

47 [50: 52: 56: 60: 64] sts.

Complete to match left front, reversing shapings.

SLEEVES

Using size 2 (2¾mm) needles cast on 55 [55: 57: 57: 59: 59] sts.

Work in rib as given for back for 8 rows, ending with RS facing for next row.

Change to size 3 (3¼mm) needles.

Beg with a K row, work in St st, shaping sides by inc 1 st at each end of 7th and every foll 8th row to 63

[73: 71: 81: 79: 89] sts, then on every foll 10th row until there are 83 [85: 87: 89: 91: 93] sts.

Work even until sleeve meas 18 [18: 18½: 18½: 19: 19] in. (46 [46: 47: 47: 48: 48]cm), ending with RS facing for next row.

Shape top

Bind off 4 [5: 5: 6: 6: 7] sts at beg of next 2 rows. 75 [75: 77: 77: 79: 79] sts.

Dec 1 st at each end of next 5 rows, then on every foll alt row until 41 sts rem, then on foll 9 rows, ending with RS facing for next row.

Bind off rem 23 sts.

FINISHING

Press as described on the information page (see page 116).

Join both shoulder seams using back stitch, or mattress stitch if preferred.

Button band

Slip 7 sts from left front holder onto size 2 (2¾mm) needles and rejoin yarn with RS facing.

Cont in rib as set until button band, when slightly stretched, fits up left front opening edge to beg of front slope shaping, ending with RS facing for next row. Bind off in rib.

Slip st band in place. Mark positions for 4 buttons on button band—first to come level with buttonhole already worked in right front, last to come just below beg of front slope shaping, and rem 2 buttons evenly spaced between.

Buttonhole band

Slip 7 sts from right front holder onto size 2 (2¾mm) needles and rejoin yarn with WS facing.

Cont in rib as set until buttonhole band, when slightly stretched, fits up right front opening edge to beg of front slope shaping, ending with RS facing for next row and with the addition of a further 3 buttonholes worked to correspond with positions marked for buttons as folls:

Buttonhole row (RS) Rib 2, work 2 tog, yo (to make a buttonhole), rib 3. When band is complete, bind off in rib. Slip st band in place.

Tie

Using size 3 (3¼mm) needles cast on 23 sts.

Row 1 (RS) K2, *P1, K1, rep from * to last st, K1.

Row 2 K1, *P1, K1, rep from * to end.

These 2 rows form rib.

Cont in rib for a further 6 rows, ending with RS facing for next row.

Row 9 (RS) Rib 5, K to last 5 sts, rib 5.

Row 10 Rib 5, P to last 5 sts, rib 5.

Rep last 2 rows until tie meas 15 in. (38cm), ending with RS facing for next row.

Place marker at beg of last row.

Next row (RS) Rib 5, K to end.

Next row P to last 5 sts, rib 5.

Rep last 2 rows until tie, from marker and unstretched, fits up entire right front slope, across back neck and down entire left front slope, beg and ending at top of band seams and ending with RS facing for next row.

Place 2nd marker at beg of last row.

Now rep rows 9 and 10 until tie meas 14 in. (36cm) from 2nd marker, ending with RS facing for next row.

Rep rows 1 and 2, 4 times, ending with RS facing for next row. Bind off in rib.

Sew row-end edge of tie between markers to neck edges.

See information page for finishing instructions, setting in sleeves using the set-in method.

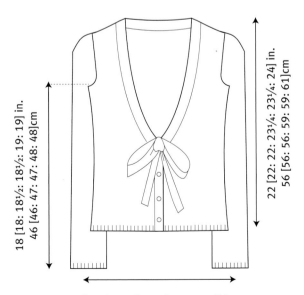

18 [18: 18½: 18½: 19: 19] in.
46 [46: 47: 47: 48: 48]cm

22 [22: 22: 23¼: 23¾: 24] in.
56 [56: 56: 59: 59: 61]cm

17 [17¾: 18½: 19¾: 21: 22¼] in.
43 [45: 47: 50: 53: 56.5]cm

lotte

See also pictures on pages 34–35.

SIZES

	S	M	L	XL	
To fit bust					
	32–34	[36–38	40–42	44–46]	in.
	81–86	[91–97	102–107	112–117]	cm

YARN

Rowan *Calmer* in Calm 461 (see page 118 for yarn information)

	9	[9	10	11]	balls

NEEDLES

1 pair size 7 (4½mm) needles
1 pair size 8 (5mm) needles
Cable needle

GAUGE

21 sts and 30 rows to 4 in. (10cm) measured over St st using size 8 (5mm) needles, *or size to obtain correct gauge.*

SPECIAL ABBREVIATIONS

C6B = slip next 3 sts onto cable needle and leave at back of work, K3, then K3 from cable needle;
C6F = slip next 3 sts onto cable needle and leave at front of work, K3, then K3 from cable needle.

BACK

Lower left panel

Using size 7 (4½mm) needles cast on 45 [47: 50: 54] sts.

Row 1 (RS) K1, P1, K12, P2, K1 [1: 0: 0], *P1, K1, rep from * to end.

Row 2 *P1, K1, rep from * to last 17 [17: 16: 16] sts, P1 [1: 0: 0], K2, P12, K2.

Row 3 K1, P1, C6B, C6F, P3 [3: 2: 2], *K1, P1, rep from * to end.

Row 4 *K1, P1, rep from * to last 17 [17: 16: 16] sts, K3 [3: 2: 2], P12, K2.

Rows 5 and 6 As rows 1 and 2.

Row 7 K1, P1, K12, P3 [3: 2: 2], *K1, P1, rep from * to end.

Row 8 As row 4.

Row 9 K1, P1, C6F, C6B, P2, K1 [1: 0: 0], *P1, K1, rep from * to end.

Row 10 As row 2.

Row 11 As row 7.

Row 12 As row 4.

These 12 rows form patt.

Work in patt for a further 14 rows, ending with RS facing for next row.

Change to size 8 (5mm) needles.

Row 27 (RS) Patt 16 sts, K to end.

Row 28 P to last 16 sts, patt to end.

These 2 rows set the sts.

Cont as set, dec 1 st at end of next and every foll 18th row until 41 [43: 46: 50] sts rem.

Work even until lower left panel meas 13½ [13¾: 14¼: 14½] in. (34 [35: 36: 37]cm), ending with WS facing for next row.

Next row (WS) P to last 16 sts, K2, (P2tog) 6 times, K2.

Break yarn and leave rem 35 [37: 40: 44] sts on a holder.

Lower center panel

Using size 7 (4½mm) needles cast on 61 [67: 73: 79] sts.

Row 1 (RS) K1, P1, K12, P2, K1, *P1, K1, rep from * to last 16 sts, P2, K12, P1, K1.

Row 2 K2, P12, K2, *P1, K1, rep from * to last 17 sts, P1, K2, P12, K2.

Row 3 K1, P1, C6B, C6F, P3, *K1, P1, rep from * to last 16 sts, P2, C6B, C6F, P1, K1.

Row 4 K2, P12, K2, *K1, P1, rep from * to last 17 sts, K3, P12, K2.

Rows 5 and 6 As rows 1 and 2.

Row 7 K1, P1, K12, P3, *K1, P1, rep from * to last 16 sts, P2, K12, P1, K1.

Row 8 As row 4.

Row 9 K1, P1, C6F, C6B, P2, K1, *P1, K1, rep from * to last 16 sts, P2, C6F, C6B, P1, K1.

Row 10 As row 2.

Row 11 As row 7.

Row 12 As row 4.

These 12 rows form patt.

Work in patt for a further 14 rows, ending with RS facing for next row.

Change to size 8 (5mm) needles.

Row 27 (RS) Patt 16 sts, K to last 16 sts, patt to end.

Row 28 Patt 16 sts, P to last 16 sts, patt to end.

These 2 rows set the sts.

Work even until lower center panel meas 13½ [13¾: 14¼: 14½] in. (34 [35: 36: 37]cm), ending with WS facing for next row.

Next row (WS) K2, (P2tog) 6 times, K2, P to last 16 sts, K2, (P2tog) 6 times, K2.

Break yarn and leave rem 49 [55: 61: 67] sts on a holder.

Lower right panel

Using size 7 (4½mm) needles cast on 45 [47: 50: 54] sts.

Row 1 (RS) *K1, P1, rep from * to last 17 [17: 16: 16] sts, K1 [1: 0: 0], P2, K12, P1, K1.

Row 2 K2, P12, K2, P1 [1: 0: 0], *K1, P1, rep from * to end.

Row 3 *P1, K1, rep from * to last 17 [17: 16: 16] sts, P3 [3: 2: 2], C6B, C6F, P1, K1.

Row 4 K2, P12, K3 [3: 2: 2], *P1, K1, rep from * to end.

Rows 5 and 6 As rows 1 and 2.

Row 7 *P1, K1, rep from * to last 17 [17: 16: 16] sts, P3 [3: 2: 2], K12, P1, K1.

Row 8 As row 4.

Row 9 *K1, P1, rep from * to last 17 [17: 16: 16] sts, K1 [1: 0: 0], P2, C6F, C6B, P1, K1.

Row 10 As row 2.

Row 11 As row 7.

Row 12 As row 4.

These 12 rows form patt.

Work in patt for a further 14 rows, ending with RS facing for next row.

Change to size 8 (5mm) needles.

Row 27 (RS) K to last 16 sts, patt to end.

Row 28 Patt 16 sts, P to end.

These 2 rows set the sts.

Cont as set, dec 1 st at beg of next and every foll 18th row until 41 [43: 46: 50] sts rem.

Work even until lower right panel meas 13½ [13¾: 14¼: 14½] in. (34 [35: 36: 37]cm), ending with WS facing for next row.

Next row (WS) K2, (P2tog) 6 times, K2, P to end. 35 [37: 40: 44] sts.

Join panels

Next row (RS) Work across lower right panel as folls P1 [1: 0: 0], (K1, P1) 12 [13: 15: 17] times, holding WS of lower center panel against RS of lower right panel K tog first st of lower center panel with next st of lower right panel, *P tog next st of center panel with next st of right panel, K tog next st of center panel with next st of right panel, rep from * 3 times more, P tog next st of center panel with last st of right panel, work across next 29 [35: 41: 47] sts of lower center panel as folls K1, (P1, K1) 14 [17: 20: 23] times, holding WS of lower center panel against RS of lower left panel P tog next st of lower center panel with first st of lower left panel, *K tog next st of center panel with next st of left panel, P tog next st of center panel with next st of left panel, rep from * 3 times more, K tog last st of center panel with next st of left panel, work across rem 25 [27: 30: 34] sts of lower left panel as folls: (P1, K1) 12 [13:

15: 17] times, P1 [1: 0: 0]. 99 [109: 121: 135] sts.
Cont in patt as folls:
Row 1 (WS) K1 [1: 0: 0], *P1, K1, rep from * to last
0 [0: 1: 1] st, P0 [0: 1: 1].
Row 2 As row 1.
Rows 3 and 4 P1 [1: 0: 0], *K1, P1, rep from * to
last 0 [0: 1: 1] st, K0 [0: 1: 1].
These 4 rows form patt.
Work 1 row, ending with RS facing for next row.
Shape raglan armholes
Keeping patt correct, bind off 3 sts at beg of next
2 rows.
93 [103: 115: 129] sts.
M, L, and XL sizes
Next row (RS) K1, skp, patt to last 3 sts, K2tog, K1.
Next row P1, P2tog, patt to last 3 sts, P2tog tbl,
P1.
Rep last 2 rows - [2: 6: 11] times more.
 - [91: 87: 81] sts.
All sizes
Next row (RS) K1, skp, patt to last 3 sts, K2tog, K1.
Next row P2, patt to last 2 sts, P2.
Rep last 2 rows 28 [27: 24: 21] times more.
Bind off rem 35 [35: 37: 37] sts.

LEFT FRONT
Using size 7 (4½mm) needles cast on 57 [62: 68:
75] sts.
Row 1 (RS) *K1, P1, rep from * to last 1 [0: 0: 1] st,
K1 [0: 0: 1].
Row 2 P1 [0: 0: 1], *K1, P1, rep from * to end.
Row 3 *P1, K1, rep from * to last 1 [0: 0: 1] st, P1
[0: 0: 1].
Row 4 K1 [0: 0: 1], *P1, K1, rep from * to end.
These 4 rows form patt.
Work in patt for a further 22 rows, ending with RS
facing for next row.
Change to size 8 (5mm) needles.
Row 27 (RS) K to last 13 sts, patt to end.
Row 28 Patt 13 sts, P to end.
These 2 rows set the sts.
Cont as set, dec 1 st at beg of next and every foll
18th row until 53 [58: 64: 71] sts rem.
Work even until left front matches back to beg of

raglan armhole shaping, ending with RS facing for
next row.
Shape raglan armhole
Next row (RS) Bind off 3 sts, K to last 13 sts and
turn, leaving rem 13 sts on a holder.
37 [42: 48: 55] sts.
Work 1 row.
Shape front slope
Working all raglan armhole decreases as given for
back, dec 1 st at raglan armhole edge of next 1 [7:
15: 25] rows, then on foll 25 [24: 21: 18] alt rows
and at same time dec 1 st at front slope edge of
next and 1 [0: 1: 0] foll 4th row, then on 7 [8: 8: 9]
foll 6th row. 2 sts.
Work 1 row, ending with RS facing for next row.
Next row (RS) K2tog and fasten off.

RIGHT FRONT
Using size 7 (4½mm) needles cast on 57 [62: 68:
75] sts.
Row 1 (RS) K1 [0: 0: 1], *P1, K1, rep from * to end.
Row 2 *P1, K1, rep from * to last 1 [0: 0: 1] st, P1
[0: 0: 1].
Row 3 P1 [0: 0: 1], *K1, P1, rep from * to end.
Row 4 *K1, P1, rep from * to last 1 [0: 0: 1] st, K1
[0: 0: 1].
These 4 rows form patt.
Work in patt for a further 22 rows, ending with RS
facing for next row.
Change to size 8 (5mm) needles.
Row 27 (RS) Patt 13 sts, K to end.
Row 28 P to last 13 sts, patt to end.
These 2 rows set the sts.
Cont as set, dec 1 st at end of next and every foll
18th row until 53 [58: 64: 71] sts rem.
Work even until right front matches back to beg of
raglan armhole shaping, ending with RS facing for
next row.
Shape raglan armhole
Next row (RS) Patt 13 sts and slip these sts onto a
holder, K to end.
Bind off 3 sts at beg of next row.
37 [42: 48: 55] sts.
Complete to match left front, reversing shapings.

SLEEVES

Using size 7 (4½mm) needles cast on 71 [73: 75: 75] sts.

Row 1 (RS) K1, *P1, K1, rep from * to end.
Rows 2 and 3 P1, *K1, P1, rep from * to end.
Row 4 As row 1.

These 4 rows form patt.

Cont in patt, dec 1 st at each end of 7th and foll 10th row.
67 [69: 71: 71] sts.

Work 5 rows, ending with RS facing for next row. (26 rows of patt completed.)

Change to size 8 (5mm) needles.

Beg with a K row, work in St st, shaping sides by dec 1 st at each end of 5th and 2 foll 10th rows.
61 [63: 65: 65] sts.

Work 7 rows, ending with RS facing for next row.

Inc 1 st at each end of next and every foll 10th [8th: 8th: 6th] row to 75 [73: 71: 73] sts, then on every foll - [10th: 10th: 8th] row until there are - [79: 81: 85] sts.

Work even until sleeve meas 17½ [17¾: 18: 18] in. (44 [45: 46: 46]cm), ending with RS facing for next row.

Shape raglan

Bind off 3 sts at beg of next 2 rows.
69 [73: 75: 79] sts.

Next row (RS) K1, skp, K to last 3 sts, K2tog, K1.
Next row P1, P2tog, P to last 3 sts, P2tog tbl, P1.
Next row K1, skp, K to last 3 sts, K2tog, K1.
Next row Purl.

Rep last 2 rows 24 [26: 27: 29] times more, ending with RS facing for next row. 15 sts.

Left sleeve only

Dec 1 st at each end of next row, then bind off 2 sts at beg of foll row. 11 sts.

Dec 1 st at beg of next row, then bind off 3 sts at beg of foll row. 7 sts.

Rep last 2 rows once more.

Right sleeve only

Bind off 3 sts at beg and dec 1 st at end of next row. 11 sts.

Work 1 row.

Rep last 2 rows twice more.

Both sleeves

Bind off rem 3 sts.

FINISHING

Press as described on the information page (see page 116).

Join raglan seams using back stitch, or mattress stitch if preferred.

Left collar

Slip 13 sts from left front holder onto size 8 (5mm) needles and rejoin yarn with RS facing.

Cont in patt as set, shaping collar by inc 1 st at beg (inner attached edge) of 3rd and foll 14 alt rows, then on every foll 4th row until there are 31 sts, taking inc sts into patt.

Work even until collar, unstretched, fits up front slope to front raglan seam, ending at outer edge.

Next row Patt to last 6 sts, wrap next st (by slipping next st from left needle to right needle, taking yarn to opposite side of work between needles and then slipping same st back onto left needle) and turn.

Next row Patt to end.

Work 2 rows.

Rep last 4 rows until shorter row-end edge of collar, unstretched, fits across top of sleeve and across to center back neck.

Bind off.

Right collar

Slip 13 sts from right front holder onto size 8 (5mm) needles and rejoin yarn with WS facing.

Cont in patt as set, shaping collar by inc 1 st at end (inner attached edge) of 2nd and foll 14 alt rows, then on every foll 4th row until there are 31 sts, taking inc sts into patt.

Complete to match left collar, reversing shaping.

Join bound-off edges of collar at center back neck, then slip st collar in place.

See information page for finishing instructions.

22 [22¾: 23½: 24½] in.
56 [58: 60: 62]cm

17½ [17¾: 18: 18] in.
44 [45: 46: 46]cm

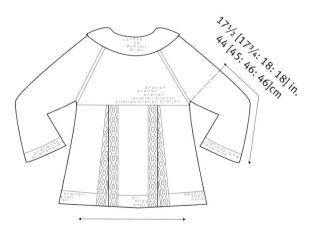

18½ [20½: 22½: 25½] in.
47 [52: 57.5: 64.5]cm

vali

See also pictures on pages 36–37.

SIZES

6	8	10	12	14	
To fit bust					
32	[34	36	38	40]	in.
81	[86	91	97	102]	cm

YARN

Rowan *Classic Cashsoft 4 ply* in Loganberry 430
(see page 118 for yarn information)

10	[11	11	12	13]	balls

NEEDLES

1 pair size 2 (2¾mm) needles
1 pair size 3 (3¼mm) needles

GAUGE

28 sts and 36 rows to 4 in. (10cm) measured over
St st using size 3 (3¼mm) needles, *or size to
obtain correct gauge.*

SPECIAL ABBREVIATIONS

Tw2 = K into front of 2nd st on left needle, then K
into front of first st, slipping both sts off left needle
together.

BACK

Using size 3 (3¼mm) needles cast on 153 [163:
163: 173: 183] sts.
Work in garter st for 2 rows, ending with RS facing
for next row.
Work in lace patt as folls:
Row 1 (RS) K1, K2tog, K3, yo, *K1, yo, K3, sl 1,
K2tog, psso, K3, yo, rep from * to last 7 sts, K1, yo,
K3, skp, K1.
Row 2 and every foll alt row Purl.
Row 3 K1, K2tog, K2, yo, *K3, yo, K2, sl 1, K2tog, psso,
K2, yo, rep from * to last 8 sts, K3, yo, K2, skp, K1.
Row 5 K1, K2tog, K1, yo, *K5, yo, K1, sl 1, K2tog,
psso, K1, yo, rep from * to last 9 sts, K5, yo, K1, skp,
K1.
Row 7 K1, K2tog, yo, K7, *yo, sl 1, K2tog, psso, yo,
K7, rep from * to last 3 sts, yo, skp, K1.
Row 9 K2, *yo, K3, sl 1, K2tog, psso, K3, yo, K1, rep
from * to last st, K1.
Row 11 K3, *yo K2, sl 1, K2tog, psso, K2, yo, K3, rep
from * to end.
Row 13 K4, *yo, K1, sl 1, K2tog, psso, K1, yo, K5, rep
from * to last 9 sts, yo, K1, sl 1, K2tog, psso, K1, yo,
K4.
Row 15 K5, *yo, sl 1, K2tog, psso, yo, K7, rep from *
to last 8 sts, yo, sl 1, K2tog, psso, yo, K5.
Row 16 Purl.
These 16 rows form patt.
Cont in patt, dec 1 st at each end of 17th and every
foll 6th row until 111 [121: 121: 131: 141] sts rem.
Work even until back meas 17¾ [17¾: 17½: 18½:
18] in. (45 [45: 44: 47: 46]cm), ending with WS
facing for next row.
Next row (WS) P10 [11: 11: 12: 13], P2tog, (P20 [22:
22: 22: 24: 26], P2tog) 4 times, P to end.
106 [116: 116: 126: 136] sts.
Next row P2, *Tw2, P3, rep from * to last 4 sts,
Tw2, P2.
Next row K2, *P2, K3, rep from * to last 4 sts,

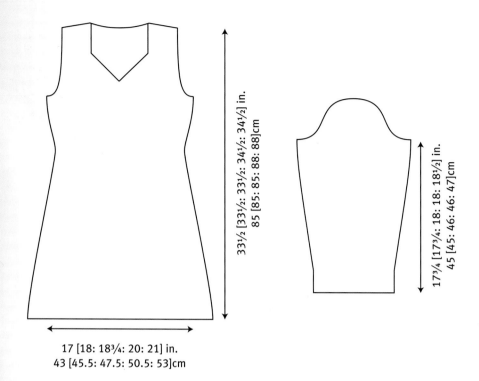

33½ [33½: 33½: 34½: 34½] in.
85 [85: 85: 88: 88]cm

17 [18: 18¾: 20: 21] in.
43 [45.5: 47.5: 50.5: 53]cm

17¾ [17¾: 18: 18: 18½] in.
45 [45: 46: 46: 47]cm

P2, K2.

These 2 rows form fancy rib.

Work in fancy rib for a further 24 rows, inc [dec: inc: inc: inc: dec] 1 [3: 3: 3: 1: 1] sts evenly across last row and ending with RS facing for next row.

107 [113: 119: 127: 135] sts.

Next row (RS) K38 [41: 44: 48: 52], P1, K5, P1, K17, P1, K5, P1, K to end.

Next row P38 [41: 44: 48: 52], K1, P5, (K1, P1) 9 times, K1, P5, K1, P to end.

Work in upper patt as folls:

Row 1 (RS) K38 [41: 44: 48: 52], P1, K1, yo K3, yo, K1, P1, K17, P1, K1, yo, K3, yo, K1, P1, K to end.

Row 2 P38 [41: 44: 48: 52], K1, P7, (K1, P1) 9 times, K1, P7, K1, P to end.

Row 3 K38 [41: 44: 48: 52], P1, K2, sl 1, K2tog, psso, K2, P1, K17, P1, K2, sl 1, K2tog, psso, K2, P1, K to end.

Row 4 P38 [41: 44: 48: 52], K1, P5, (K1, P1) 9 times, K1, P5, K1, P to end.

These 4 rows form upper patt. (Note: Number of sts varies whilst working upper patt. All st counts given

presume there are 31 sts in center panel at all times.)

Cont in upper patt, inc 1 st at each end of next and every foll 4th row until there are 121 [127: 133: 141: 149] sts, taking inc sts into St st.

Work even until back meas 25½ [25½: 25¼: 26½: 26] in. (65 [65: 64: 67: 66]cm), ending with RS facing for next row.

Shape armholes

Keeping patt correct, bind off 5 [6: 6: 7: 7] sts at beg of next 2 rows. 111 [115: 121: 127: 135] sts.**

Dec 1 st at each end of next 5 [5: 7: 7: 9] rows, then on foll 4 [5: 4: 5: 5] alt rows.

93 [95: 99: 103: 107] sts.

Work even until armhole meas 8 [8: 8¼: 8¼: 8¾] in. (20 [20: 21: 21: 22]cm), ending with RS facing for next row.

Shape shoulders and back neck

Bind off 7 [7: 8: 8: 9] sts at beg of next 2 rows. 79 [81: 83: 87: 89] sts.

Next row (RS) Bind off 7 [7: 8: 8: 9] sts, patt until there are 10 [11: 11: 13: 12] sts on right needle and turn, leaving rem sts on a holder.

Work each side of neck separately.

Bind off 4 sts at beg of next row.

Bind off rem 6 [7: 7: 9: 8] sts.

With RS facing, rejoin yarn to rem sts, bind off center 45 [45: 45: 45: 47] sts, patt to end.

Complete to match first side, reversing shapings.

FRONT

Work as given for back to **.

Dec 1 st at each end of next 5 [5: 6: 6: 6] rows. 101 [105: 109: 115: 123] sts.

Work 1 [1: 0: 0: 0] row, ending with RS facing for next row.

Divide for neck

Next row (RS) K2tog, patt 48 [50: 52: 55: 59] sts and turn, leaving rem sts on a holder.

Work each side of neck separately.

Dec 0 [0: 0: 0: 1] st at armhole edge of next row. 49 [51: 53: 56: 59] sts.

Dec 1 st at neck edge of next and foll 24 [24: 22: 22: 22] rows, then on 1 [1: 3: 3: 4] foll 4th rows and at same time dec 1 st at armhole edge of next and foll 2 [3: 3: 4: 5] alt rows. 20 [21: 23: 25: 26] sts.

Work even until front matches back to beg of shoulder shaping, ending with RS facing for next row.

Shape shoulder

Bind off 7 [7: 8: 8: 9] sts at beg of next and foll alt row.

Work 1 row.

Bind off rem 6 [7: 7: 9: 8] sts.

With RS facing, rejoin yarn to rem sts, K2tog, patt to last 2 sts, K2tog.

Complete to match first side, reversing shapings.

SLEEVES

Using size 2 (2¾mm) needles cast on 71 [71: 73: 73: 75] sts.

Row 1 (RS) P2 [2: 3: 3: 4], Tw2, *P3, Tw2, rep from * to last 2 [2: 3: 3: 4] sts, P2 [2: 3: 3: 4].

Row 2 K2 [2: 3: 3: 4], P2, *K3, P2, rep from * to last 2 [2: 3: 3: 4] sts, K2 [2: 3: 3: 4].

These 2 rows form fancy rib.

Work in fancy rib for a further 24 rows, inc 1 st at center of last row and ending with RS facing for next row. 72 [72: 74: 74: 76] sts.

Change to size 3 (3¼mm) needles.

Beg with a K row, work in St st, shaping sides by inc 1 st at each end of next and every foll 10th [10th: 10th: 8th: 8th] row to 76 [88: 98: 84: 92] sts, then on every foll 12th [12th: 12th: 10th: 10th] row until there are 94 [96: 100: 102: 106] sts.

Work even until sleeve meas 17¾ [17¾: 18: 18: 18½] in. (45 [45: 46: 46: 47]cm), ending with RS facing for next row.

Shape top

Bind off 5 [6: 6: 7: 7] sts at beg of next 2 rows. 84 [84: 88: 88: 92] sts.

Dec 1 st at each end of next 5 rows, then on every foll alt row to 50 sts, then on foll 13 rows, ending with RS facing for next row.

Bind off rem 24 sts.

FINISHING

Press as described on the information page (see page 116).

Join right shoulder seam using back stitch, or mattress stitch if preferred.

Neckband

With RS facing and using size 2 (2¾mm) needles, pick up and knit 64 [64: 68: 68: 72] sts down left side of neck, place marker on needle, pick up and knit 64 [64: 68: 68: 72] sts up right side of neck, then 52 [52: 53: 53: 54] sts from back. 180 [180: 189: 189: 198] sts.

Row 1 (WS) K to within 2 sts of marker, K2tog, slip marker onto right needle, K2tog tbl, K to end.

Rep this row 3 times more, ending with WS facing for next row. 172 [172: 181: 181: 190] sts.

Work picot cast-on (on WS) as folls: bind off 2 sts, *slip st now on right needle back onto left needle, cast on 2 sts, bind off 5 sts, rep from * until all sts have been bound off, ending last rep with bind off rem 4 sts.

See information page for finishing instructions, setting in sleeves using the set-in method.

slouchy

See also pictures on pages 38–39.

SIZES

6	8	10	12	14	16	
To fit bust						
32	[34	36	38	40	42]	in.
81	[86	91	97	102	107]	cm

YARN

Rowan *Kidsilk Haze* (see page 118 for yarn
information)

A Cream 634

3	[3	3	4	4	4]	balls

B Ghost 642

3	[3	3	4	4	4]	balls

NEEDLES

1 pair size 9 (5½mm) needles

GAUGE

18 sts and 21 rows to 4 in. (10cm) measured over
St st using size 9 (5½mm) needles, *or size to
obtain correct gauge,* and one strand each of yarn A
and B held together.

BACK

Using size 9 (5½mm) needles and yarns A and B
held together cast on 82 [86: 90: 96: 100: 106] sts.
Work in garter st for 4 rows, ending with RS facing
for next row.
Beg with a K row, work in St st until back meas 10½
[10½: 10¼: 11½: 11: 12] in. (27 [27: 26: 29: 28:
30]cm), ending with RS facing for next row.

Shape for cap sleeves

Inc 1 st at each end of next and foll 5 alt rows.
94 [98: 102: 108: 112: 118] sts.
Cast on 19 [19: 21: 21: 23: 23] sts at beg of next
2 rows. 132 [136: 144: 150: 158: 164] sts.**
Work even until work meas 9½ [9½: 10: 10: 10¼:
10¼] in. (24 [24: 25: 25: 26: 26]cm) from last set of
cast-on sts, ending with RS facing for next row.

Shape shoulders and back neck

Next row (RS) Bind off 21 [22: 24: 26: 27: 29] sts,
K until there are 25 [26: 28: 29: 31: 32] sts on right
needle and turn, leaving rem sts on a holder.
Work each side of neck separately.
Bind off 3 sts at beg of next row.
Bind off rem 22 [23: 25: 26: 28: 29] sts.
With RS facing, rejoin yarns to rem sts, bind off
center 40 [40: 40: 40: 42: 42] sts, K to end.
Complete to match first side, reversing shapings.

FRONT

Work as given for back to **.
Work even until work meas 5½ [5½: 6: 5½: 6: 6] in.
(14 [14: 15: 14: 15: 15]cm) from last set of cast-on
sts, ending with RS facing for next row.

Shape neck

Next row (RS) K48 [50: 54: 58: 61: 64] and turn,
leaving rem sts on a holder.
Work each side of neck separately.
Dec 1 st at neck edge of 2nd and foll 4 [4: 4: 5:
5: 5] alt rows. 43 [45: 49: 52: 55: 58] sts.
Work even until front matches back to beg of
shoulder shaping, ending with RS facing for next row.

Shape shoulder

Bind off 21 [22: 24: 26: 27: 29] sts at beg of next row.

Work 1 row.

Bind off rem 22 [23: 25: 26: 28: 29] sts.

With RS facing, rejoin yarns to rem sts, bind off center 36 [36: 36: 34: 36: 36] sts, K to end.

Complete to match first side, reversing shapings.

FINISHING

Press as described on the information page (see page 116).

Join right shoulder and overarm seam using back stitch, or mattress stitch if preferred.

Neckband

With RS facing, using size 9 (5½mm) needles and yarns A and B held together, pick up and knit 22 [22: 22: 24: 24: 24] sts down left side of neck, 36 [36: 36: 34: 36: 36] sts from front, 22 [22: 22: 24: 24: 24] sts up right side of neck, then 45 [45: 45: 45: 47: 47] sts from back.

125 [125: 125: 127: 131: 131] sts.

Bind off knitwise (on WS).

See information page for finishing instructions.

Using photograph as a guide, fold 2 in. (5cm) cuff to RS and stitch in place at seams.

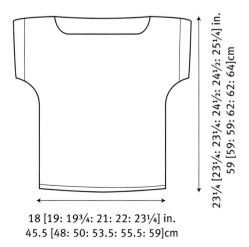

23¼ [23¼: 23¾: 24½: 24½: 25¼] in.
59 [59: 59: 62: 62: 64]cm

18 [19: 19¾: 21: 22: 23¼] in.
45.5 [48: 50: 53.5: 55.5: 59]cm

sweetheart

See also pictures on pages 40–41.

SIZES

6	8	10	12	14	16	
To fit bust						
32	[34	36	38	40	42]	in.
81	[86	91	97	102	107]	cm

YARN

Rowan *Kidsilk Haze* in Liqueur 595 (see page 118 for yarn information)

5	[5	5	6	6	6]	balls

NEEDLES

1 pair size 2 (2¾mm) needles
1 pair size 3 (3¼mm) needles

BUTTONS

11 x hexagonal buttons, ½ in. (15mm) in diameter

GAUGE

25 sts and 34 rows to 4 in. (10cm) measured over St st using size 3 (3¼mm) needles, *or size to obtain correct gauge.*

BACK

Using size 2 (2¾mm) needles cast on 107 [113: 117: 125: 133: 141] sts.
Row 1 (RS) K1, *P1, K1, rep from * to end.
Row 2 As row 1.
These 2 rows form seed st.
Work in seed st for a further 6 rows, ending with RS facing for next row.
Change to size 3 (3¼mm) needles.

Beg with a K row, work in St st for 12 rows, ending with RS facing for next row.
Next row (dec) (RS) K2, skp, K to last 4 sts, K2tog, K2.
Working all side seam decreases as set by last row, dec 1 st at each end of 12th and 2 foll 10th rows.
99 [105: 109: 117: 125: 133] sts.
Work 15 rows, ending with RS facing for next row.
Next row (inc) (RS) K3, M1, K to last 3 sts, M1, K3.
Working all side seam increases as set by last row, inc 1 st at each end of 12th and 2 foll 12th rows.
107 [113: 117: 125: 133: 141] sts.
Work even until back meas 13¾ [13¾: 13½: 14½: 14¼: 15] in. (35 [35: 34: 37: 36: 38]cm), ending with RS facing for next row.
Shape armholes
Bind off 4 [5: 5: 6: 6: 7] sts at beg of next 2 rows.
99 [103: 107: 113: 121: 127] sts.
Next row (RS) K2, skp, K to last 4 sts, K2tog, K2.
Next row P2, P2tog, P to last 4 sts, P2tog tbl, P2.
Working all armhole decreases as set by last 2 rows, dec 1 st at each end of next 1 [1: 3: 3: 5: 5] rows, then on foll 5 [6: 5: 6: 6: 7] alt rows.
83 [85: 87: 91: 95: 99] sts.
Work even until armhole meas 7½ [7½: 8: 8: 8¼: 8¼] in. (19 [19: 20: 20: 21: 21]cm), ending with RS facing for next row.
Shape shoulders and back neck
Bind off 6 [6: 7: 7: 8: 8] sts at beg of next 2 rows.
71 [73: 73: 77: 79: 83] sts.
Next row (RS) Bind off 6 [6: 7: 7: 8: 8] sts, K until there are 10 [11: 10: 12: 11: 13] sts on right needle and turn, leaving rem sts on a holder.

Work each side of neck separately.

Bind off 4 sts at beg of next row.

Bind off rem 6 [7: 6: 8: 7: 9] sts.

With RS facing, rejoin yarn to rem sts, bind off center 39 [39: 39: 39: 41: 41] sts, K to end.

Complete to match first side, reversing shapings.

LEFT FRONT

Using size 2 (2¾mm) needles cast on 57 [61: 63: 67: 71: 75] sts.

Work in seed st as given for back for 7 rows, ending with WS facing for next row.

Row 8 (WS) Seed st 7 sts and slip these sts onto a holder, M1, seed st to last 0 [2: 2: 2: 2: 2] sts, (work 2 tog) 0 [1: 1: 1: 1: 1] times.

51 [54: 56: 60: 64: 68] sts.

Change to size 3 (3¼mm) needles.

Beg with a K row, work in St st for 12 rows, ending with RS facing for next row.

Working all side seam decreases as set by back, dec 1 st at beg of next and foll 12th row, then on 2 foll 10th rows. 47 [50: 52: 56: 60: 64] sts.

Work 15 rows, ending with RS facing for next row.

Working all side seam increases as set by back, inc 1 st at beg of next and 3 foll 12th rows.

51 [54: 56: 60: 64: 68] sts.

Work even until left front matches back to beg of armhole shaping, ending with RS facing for next row.

Shape armhole and front neck

Bind off 4 [5: 5: 6: 6: 7] sts at beg and dec 1 st at end of next row. 46 [48: 50: 53: 57: 60] sts.

Dec 1 st at neck edge of next row.

45 [47: 49: 52: 56: 59] sts.

Working all armhole decreases as set by back, dec 1 st at armhole edge of next 3 [3: 5: 5: 7: 7] rows, then on foll 5 [6: 5: 6: 6: 7] alt rows and at same time dec 1 st at neck edge of next 13 [15: 13: 13: 11: 11] rows, then on foll 0 [0: 1: 2: 4: 5] alt rows.

24 [23: 25: 26: 28: 29] sts.

Dec 1 st at neck edge only on next [2nd: 2nd: 2nd: 2nd: 2nd] and foll 1 [0: 0: 0: 0: 0] rows, then on foll 4 [3: 4: 3: 4: 3] alt rows, ending with WS facing for next row. 18 [19: 20: 22: 23: 25] sts.

Place marker at neck edge of last row.

Work even until left front matches back to beg of shoulder shaping, ending with RS facing for next row.

Shape shoulder

Bind off 6 [6: 7: 7: 8: 8] sts at beg of next and foll alt row.

Work 1 row.

Bind off rem 6 [7: 6: 8: 7: 9] sts.

RIGHT FRONT

Using size 2 (2¾mm) needles cast on 57 [61: 63: 67: 71: 75] sts.

Work in seed st as given for back for 4 rows, ending with RS facing for next row.

Row 5 (RS) Seed st 2 sts, K2tog, yo (to make first buttonhole), seed st to end.

Work in seed st for 2 more rows, ending with WS facing for next row.

Row 8 (WS) (Work 2 tog) 0 [1: 1: 1: 1: 1] times, seed st to last 7 sts, M1 and turn, leaving rem 7 sts on a holder. 51 [54: 56: 60: 64: 68] sts.

Change to size 3 (3¼mm) needles.

Beg with a K row, work in St st for 12 rows, ending with RS facing for next row.

Working all side seam decreases as set by back, dec 1 st at end of next and foll 12th row, then on 2 foll 10th rows.

47 [50: 52: 56: 60: 64] sts.

Complete to match left front, reversing shapings.

LEFT SLEEVE

Front section

Using size 2 (2¾mm) needles cast on 37 [37: 39: 39: 41: 41] sts.

Work in seed st as given for back for 4 rows, ending with RS facing for next row.

Row 5 (RS) Seed st 2 sts, K2tog, yo (to make first buttonhole), seed st to end.

Work in seed st for 3 more rows, ending with RS facing for next row.

Change to size 3 (3¼mm) needles.

Row 9 (RS) Seed st 7 sts, K to end.

Row 10 P to last 7 sts, seed st to end.

These 2 rows set the sts.

Working all increases as set by side seam increases,

work 6 rows, inc 1 st at end of 5th of these rows. 38 [38: 40: 40: 42: 42] sts.

Row 17 (RS) Seed st 2 sts, K2tog, yo (to make 2nd buttonhole), seed st 3 sts, K to end.

Work 11 rows, inc 1 st at end of 6th of these rows. 39 [39: 41: 41: 43: 43] sts.

Row 29 (RS) As row 17 (to make 3rd buttonhole).

Work 11 rows, inc 1 st at end of 2nd and foll 8th of these rows and ending with RS facing for next row. 41 [41: 43: 43: 45: 45] sts.

Break yarn and leave sts on a holder.

Back section

Using size 2 (2¾mm) needles cast on 25 sts.

Work in seed st as given for back for 8 rows, ending with RS facing for next row.

Change to size 3 (3¼mm) needles.

Row 9 (RS) K to last 7 sts, seed st to end.

Row 10 Seed st 7 sts, P to end.

These 2 rows set the sts.

Working all increases as set by side seam increases, inc 1 st at beg of 5th and 3 foll 8th rows. 29 sts.

Work 1 row, ending with RS facing for next row.

Join sections.

Next row (RS) K first 22 sts of back section, holding WS of front section against RS of back section K tog first st of front section with next st of back section, (K tog next st of front section with next st of back section) 6 times, K rem 34 [34: 36: 36: 38: 38] sts of front section. 63 [63: 65: 65: 67: 67] sts.

**Beg with a P row, work in St st, shaping sides by inc 1 st at each end of 8th [6th: 6th: 6th: 6th: 6th] and 0 [4: 2: 7: 5: 10] foll 8th rows, then on every foll 10th row until there are 83 [85: 87: 89: 91: 93] sts.

Work even until sleeve meas 18 [18: 18½: 18½: 19: 19] in. (46 [46: 47: 47: 48: 48]cm), ending with RS facing for next row.

Shape top

Bind off 4 [5: 5: 6: 6: 7] sts at beg of next 2 rows. 75 [75: 77: 77: 79: 79] sts.

Dec 1 st at each end of next 5 rows, then on every foll alt row until 41 sts rem, then on foll 9 rows, ending with RS facing for next row.

Bind off rem 23 sts.

RIGHT SLEEVE

Back section

Using size 2 (2¾mm) needles cast on 25 sts.

Work in seed st as given for back for 8 rows, ending with RS facing for next row.

Change to size 3 (3¼mm) needles.

Row 9 (RS) Seed st 7 sts, K to end.

Row 10 P to last 7 sts, seed st to end.

These 2 rows set the sts.

Working all increases as set by side seam increases, inc 1 st at end of 5th and 3 foll 8th rows. 29 sts.

Work 1 row, ending with RS facing for next row.

Break yarn and leave sts on a holder.

Front section

Using size 2 (2¾mm) needles cast on 37 [37: 39: 39: 41: 41] sts.

Work in seed st as given for back for 4 rows, ending with RS facing for next row.

Row 5 (RS) Seed st to last 4 sts, yo, K2tog (to make first buttonhole), seed st 2 sts.

Work in seed st for 3 more rows, ending with RS facing for next row.

Change to size 3 (3¼mm) needles.

Row 9 (RS) K to last 7 sts, seed st to end.

Row 10 Seed st 7 sts, P to end.

These 2 rows set the sts.

Working all increases as set by side seam increases, work 6 rows, inc 1 st at beg of 5th of these rows. 38 [38: 40: 40: 42: 42] sts.

Row 17 (RS) Seed st to last 7 sts, seed st 3 sts, yo, K2tog (to make 2nd buttonhole), seed st 2 sts.

Work 11 rows, inc 1 st at beg of 6th of these rows. 39 [39: 41: 41: 43: 43] sts.

Row 29 (RS) As row 17 (to make 3rd buttonhole).

Work 11 rows, inc 1 st at beg of 2nd and foll 8th of these rows and ending with RS facing for next row. 41 [41: 43: 43: 45: 45] sts.

Join sections

Next row (RS) K first 34 [34: 36: 36: 38: 38] sts of front section, holding WS of front section against RS of back section K tog next st of front section with first st of back section, (K tog next st of front section with next st of back section) 6 times, K rem 22 sts of back section.

63 [63: 65: 65: 67: 67] sts.

Complete as given for left sleeve from **.

FINISHING

Press as described on the information page (see page 116).

Join both shoulder seams using back stitch, or mattress stitch if preferred.

Button band

Slip 7 sts from left front holder onto size 2 (2¾mm) needles and rejoin yarn with RS facing.

Cont in seed st as set until button band, when slightly stretched, fits up left front opening edge to beg of neck shaping, ending with RS facing for next row.

Break yarn and slip sts onto a holder.

Slip st band in place. Mark positions for 5 buttons on button band—first to come level with buttonhole already worked in right front, last to come just above neck shaping, and rem 3 buttons evenly spaced between.

Buttonhole band

Slip 7 sts from right front holder onto size 2 (2¾mm) needles and rejoin yarn with WS facing.

Cont in seed st as set until buttonhole band, when slightly stretched, fits up right front opening edge to beg of neck shaping, ending with RS facing for next row and with the addition of a further 3 buttonholes worked to correspond with positions marked for buttons as folls:

Buttonhole row (RS) Seed st 2 sts, K2tog, yo, seed st 3 sts.

When band is complete, do NOT break yarn.

Slip st band in place.

Neckband

With RS facing and using size 2 (2¾mm) needles, seed st across 7 sts of buttonhole band, pick up and knit 25 [25: 27: 27: 31: 31] sts up right side of neck to marker, 1 st at marker (mark this st with a colored thread), 35 sts up straight row-end edge to shoulder, 47 [47: 47: 47: 49: 49] sts from back, 35 sts down straight row-end edge to other marker, 1 st at marker (mark this st with a colored thread), and 25 [25: 27: 27: 31: 31] sts down left side of neck, then seed st 7 sts of button band.

183 [183: 187: 187: 197: 197] sts.

Work in seed st as set by bands for 1 row, ending with RS facing for next row.

Row 2 (RS) *Seed st to within 2 sts of marked st, work 2 tog, K marked st, work 2 tog, rep from * once more, seed st to end.

179 [179: 183: 183: 193: 193] sts.

Row 3 *Seed st to marked st, P marked st, rep from * once more, seed st to end.

Row 4 Seed st 2 sts, K2tog, yo (to make last buttonhole), *seed st to within 2 sts of marked st, work 2 tog, K marked st, work 2 tog, rep from * once more, seed st to end.

175 [175: 179: 179: 189: 189] sts.

Row 5 As row 3.

Rows 6 and 7 As rows 2 and 3.

171 [171: 175: 175: 185: 185] sts.

Bind off in seed st, still dec either side of marked sts as before.

See information page for finishing instructions, setting in sleeves using the set-in method and attaching buttons to back sections of sleeves to correspond with buttonholes in front sections.

18 [18: 18½: 18½: 19: 19] in.
46 [46: 47: 47: 48: 48]cm

22 [22: 22: 23¾: 23¾: 24] in.
56 [56: 56: 59: 59: 61]cm

17 [17¾: 18½: 19¾: 21: 22¼] in.
43 [45: 47: 50: 53: 56.5]cm

malin

See also pictures on pages 42–43.

See also pictures on pages 42–43.

SIZES

	S	M	L	XL	
To fit bust					
	32–34	[36–38	40–42	44–46]	in.
	81–86	[91–97	102–107	112–117]	cm

YARN

Rowan *Kidsilk Haze* in Pearl 590 (see page 118 for yarn information)

	3	[4	4	5]	balls

NEEDLES

1 pair size 3 (3¼mm) needles
1 pair size 6 (4mm) needles

GAUGE

20 sts and 31 rows to 4 in. (10cm) measured over 16 row patt rep (chart, page 107) using size 6 (4mm) needles, *or size to obtain correct gauge*.

BACK

Using size 6 (4mm) needles cast on 105 [115: 127: 139] sts.
Work in garter st for 4 rows, ending with RS facing for next row.
Beg with a K row, work in St st for 2 rows, ending with RS facing for next row.
Beg and ending rows as indicated, working chart rows 1 and 2 once only and then repeating chart rows 3 to 18 throughout, cont in 16 row patt rep from chart for body as folls:
Work 54 rows, ending with RS facing for next row.

Keeping patt correct, dec 1 st at each end of next and foll 20th row.
101 [111: 123: 135] sts.
Work even until back meas 13¾ [14¼: 14½: 15] in. (35 [36: 37: 38]cm), ending with RS facing for next row.

Shape armholes

Keeping patt correct, bind off 6 [7: 8: 9] sts at beg of next 2 rows.
89 [97: 107: 117] sts.
Dec 1 st at each end of next 5 [7: 9: 11] rows, then on foll 3 alt rows.
73 [77: 83: 89] sts.
Work even until armhole meas 8 [8¼: 8¾: 9] in. (20 [21: 22: 23]cm), ending with RS facing for next row.

Shape back neck and shoulders

Next row (RS) Patt 20 [22: 24: 27] sts and turn, leaving rem sts on a holder.
Work each side of neck separately.
Bind off 3 sts at beg of next row, 7 [8: 9: 10] sts at beg of foll row, then 3 sts at beg of next row.
Bind off rem 7 [8: 9: 11] sts.
With RS facing, slip center 33 [33: 35: 35] sts onto a holder, rejoin yarn to rem sts, patt to end.
Complete to match first side, reversing shapings.

FRONT

Work as given for back until 32 [32: 34: 34] rows less have been worked than on back to beg of shoulder shaping ending with RS facing for next row.

16 row patt repeat

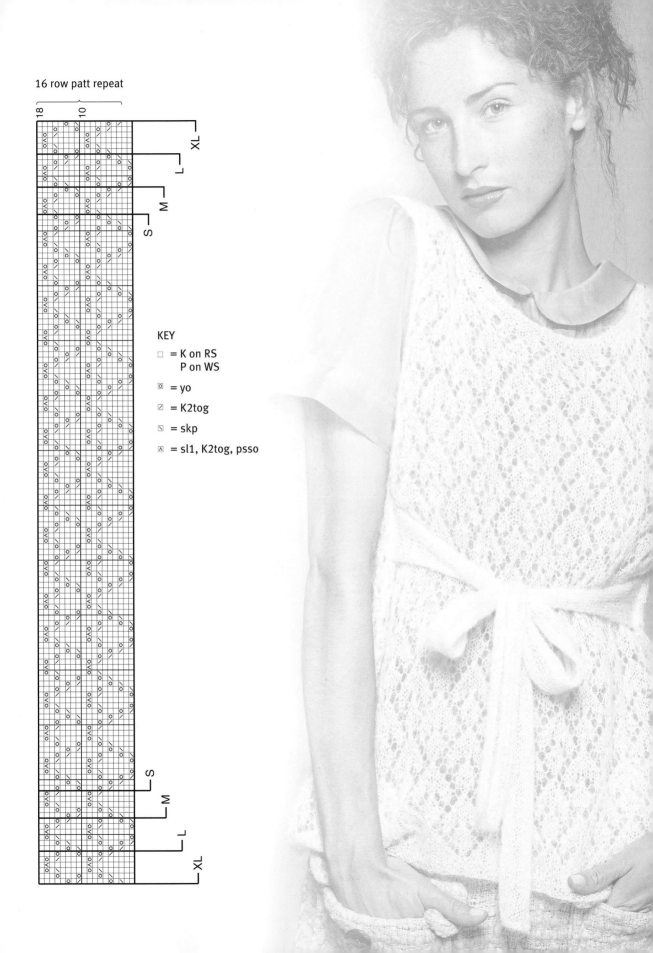

KEY

□ = K on RS
P on WS

◉ = yo

⊠ = K2tog

⧅ = skp

⧆ = sl1, K2tog, psso

Shape neck

Next row (RS) Patt 27 [29: 32: 35] sts and turn, leaving rem sts on a holder.

Work each side of neck separately.

Keeping patt correct, dec 1 st at neck edge of next 6 rows, then on foll 7 [7: 8: 8] alt rows.

14 [16: 18: 21] sts.

Work 11 rows, ending with RS facing for next row.

Shape shoulder

Bind off 7 [8: 9: 10] sts at beg of next row.

Work 1 row.

Bind off rem 7 [8: 9: 11] sts.

With RS facing, slip center 19 sts onto a holder, rejoin yarn to rem sts, patt to end.

Complete to match first side, reversing shapings.

FINISHING

Press as described on the information page (see page 116).

Join right shoulder seam using back stitch, or mattress stitch if preferred.

Neckband

With RS facing and using size 3 (3¼mm) needles, pick up and knit 32 [32: 34: 34] sts down left side of front neck, K 19 sts from front holder, pick up and knit 32 [32: 34: 34] sts up right side of front neck, and 5 sts down right side of back neck, K 33 [33: 35: 35] sts from back, then pick up and knit 5 sts up left side of back neck.

126 [126: 132: 132] sts.

Work in garter st for 4 rows, ending with WS facing for next row.

Bind off knitwise (on WS).

Join left shoulder and neckband seam.

Armhole borders (both alike)

With RS facing and using size 3 (3¼mm) needles, pick up and knit 124 [130: 136: 142] sts evenly all round armhole edge.

Work in garter st for 4 rows, ending with WS facing for next row.

Bind off knitwise (on WS).

Ties (make 2)

Using size 6 (4mm) needles cast on 16 sts.

Beg with a K row, work in St st for 22¾ [23½: 24½: 25¼] in. (58 [60: 62: 64]cm), ending with RS facing for next row.

Bind off.

See information page for finishing instructions, enclosing cast-on ends of ties in side seams approx 2½ in. (6cm) below underarm.

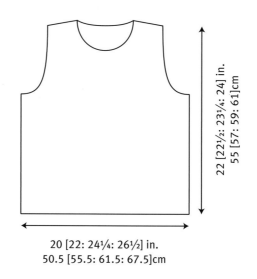

20 [22: 24¼: 26½] in.
50.5 [55.5: 61.5: 67.5]cm

22 [22½: 23¼: 24] in.
55 [57: 59: 61]cm

griselda

See also pictures on pages 44–45.

SIZES

6	8	10	12	14	16	
To fit bust						
32	[34	36	38	40	42]	in.
81	[86	91	97	102	107]	cm

YARN

Rowan *Wool Cotton* in Antique 900 (see page 118 for yarn information)

9	[10	10	11	11	12]	balls

NEEDLES

1 pair size 3 (3¼mm) needles
1 pair size 6 (4mm) needles
Size 3 (3¼mm) circular needle
Cable needle

BUTTONS

2 x bone buttons, ½ in. (12mm) in diameter

GAUGE

22 sts and 30 rows to 4 in. (10cm) measured over St st using size 6 (4mm) needles, *or size to obtain correct gauge.*

SPECIAL ABBREVIATIONS

C3B = slip next 2 sts onto cable needle and leave at back of work, K1, then K2 from cable needle.

BACK

Using size 3 (3¼mm) needles cast on 100 [105: 110: 115: 125: 130] sts.

Row 1 (RS) P1, *K3, P2, rep from * to last 4 sts, K3, P1.

Row 2 K1, *P3, K2, rep from * to last 4 sts, P3, K1.

Row 3 P1, *C3B, P2, rep from * to last 4 sts, C3B, P1.

Row 4 As row 2.

These 4 rows form fancy rib.

Work in fancy rib for a further 23 rows, ending with WS facing for next row.

Row 28 (WS) Rib 16 [12: 10: 13: 9: 12], work 2 tog, (rib 31 [24: 20: 27: 19: 24], work 2 tog) 2 [3: 4: 3: 5: 4] times, rib 16 [13: 10: 13: 9: 12].

97 [101: 105: 111: 119: 125] sts.

Change to size 6 (4mm) needles.

Beg with a K row, work in St st, dec 1 st at each end of 5th and 2 foll 6th rows.

91 [95: 99: 105: 113: 119] sts.

Work 15 rows, ending with RS facing for next row.

Inc 1 st at each end of next and 2 foll 10th rows.

97 [101: 105: 111: 119: 125] sts.

Work even until back meas 13¾ [13¾: 13½: 14½: 14¼: 15] in. (35 [35: 34: 37: 36: 38]cm), ending with RS facing for next row.

Shape armholes

Bind off 5 [6: 6: 7: 7: 8] sts at beg of next 2 rows.

87 [89: 93: 97: 105: 109] sts.

Dec 1 st at each end of next 3 [3: 5: 5: 7: 7] rows, then on foll 3 [3: 2: 2: 3: 3] alt rows.

75 [77: 79: 83: 85: 89] sts.

Work even until armhole meas 8¼ [8¼: 8¾: 8¾: 9: 9] in. (21 [21: 22: 22: 23: 23]cm), ending with RS facing for next row.

Shape shoulders and back neck

Next row (RS) Bind off 7 [8: 8: 9: 9: 10] sts, K until there are 12 [12: 13: 14: 14: 15] sts on right needle and turn, leaving rem sts on a holder.

Work each side of neck separately.

Bind off 4 sts at beg of next row.

Bind off rem 8 [8: 9: 10: 10: 11] sts.

With RS facing, rejoin yarn to rem sts, bind off center 37 [37: 37: 37: 39: 39] sts, K to end.

Complete to match first side, reversing shapings.

FRONT

Work as given for back until 10 rows less have been worked than on back to beg of armhole shaping, ending with RS facing for next row.

Divide for front opening

Next row (RS) K45 [47: 49: 52: 56: 59] and turn, leaving rem sts on a holder.

Work each side of neck separately.

Work 9 rows, ending with RS facing for next row.

Shape armhole

Bind off 5 [6: 6: 7: 7: 8] sts at beg of next row.

40 [41: 43: 45: 49: 51] sts.

Work 1 row.

Dec 1 st at armhole edge of next 3 [3: 5: 5: 7: 7] rows, then on foll 3 [3: 2: 2: 3: 3] alt rows.

34 [35: 36: 38: 39: 41] sts.

Work 9 [9: 9: 9: 5: 5] rows, ending with RS facing for next row.

Shape front slope

Dec 1 st at end of next row and at same edge on foll 2 [2: 0: 0: 0: 0] rows, then on foll 16 [16: 18: 18: 18: 18] alt rows, then on 0 [0: 0: 0: 1: 1] foll 4th row.

15 [16: 17: 19: 19: 21] sts.

Work even until front matches back to beg of shoulder shaping, ending with RS facing for next row.

Shape shoulder

Bind off 7 [8: 8: 9: 9: 10] sts at beg of next row.

Work 1 row.

Bind off rem 8 [8: 9: 10: 10: 11] sts.

With RS facing, rejoin yarn to rem sts, bind off center 7 sts, K to end.

Complete to match first side, reversing shapings.

SLEEVES

Using size 3 (3¼mm) needles cast on 50 sts.

Work in fancy rib as given for back for 19 rows, ending with WS facing for next row.

Row 20 (WS) Rib 4 [4: 7: 7: 24: 24], work 2 tog, (rib 8 [8: 15: 15: -: -], work 2 tog) 4 [4: 2: 2: 0: 0] times, rib 4 [4: 7: 7: 24: 24].

45 [45: 47: 47: 49: 49] sts.

Change to size 6 (4mm) needles.

Beg with a K row, work in St st, shaping sides by inc 1 st at each end of 5th and every foll 6th row to 51 [59: 59: 67: 65: 73] sts, then on every foll 8th row until there are 73 [75: 77: 79: 81: 83] sts.

Work even until sleeve meas 18 [18: 18½: 18½: 19: 19] in. (46 [46: 47: 47: 48: 48]cm), ending with RS facing for next row.

Shape top

Bind off 5 [6: 6: 7: 7: 8] sts at beg of next 2 rows.

63 [63: 65: 65: 67: 67] sts.

Dec 1 st at each end of next and foll 5 alt rows, then on 3 foll 4th rows, then on every foll alt row until 31 sts rem, then on foll 3 rows, ending with RS facing for next row.

Bind off rem 25 sts.

FINISHING

Press as described on the information page (see page 116).

Join both shoulder seams using back stitch, or mattress stitch if preferred.

Neckband

With RS facing and using size 3 (3¼mm) circular needle, beg and ending at base of front opening, pick up and knit 27 sts up right front opening edge to beg of front slope shaping, 43 [43: 45: 45: 47: 47] sts up right front slope, 45 [45: 46: 46: 47: 47] sts from back, 43 [43: 45: 45: 47: 47] sts down left front slope to beg of front slope shaping, then 27 sts down left front opening edge.

185 [185: 190: 190: 195: 195] sts.

Beg with row 2, work in fancy rib as given for back for 5 rows, ending with RS facing for next row.

Row 6 (RS) Rib 10, bind off 2 sts (to make a buttonhole—cast on 2 sts over these bound-off sts on next row), rib until there are 10 sts on right needle after bind-off, bind off 2 sts (to make 2nd buttonhole—cast on 2 sts over these bound-off sts on next row), rib to end.

Work a further 5 rows, ending with RS facing for next row.

Bind off in rib.

Slip st row-end edges of neckband to bound-off sts at base of front opening, ensuring end with buttonholes in is on top. See information page for finishing instructions, setting in sleeves using the set-in method.

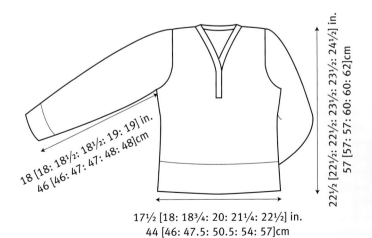

18 [18: 18½: 18½: 19: 19] in.
46 [46: 47: 47: 48: 48]cm

17½ [18: 18¾: 20: 21¼: 22½] in.
44 [46: 47.5: 50.5: 54: 57]cm

22½ [22½: 22½: 23½: 23½: 24½] in.
57 [57: 57: 60: 60: 62]cm

lucille

See also pictures on pages 46–47.

SIZES

6	8	10	12	14	16

To fit bust

32	[34	36	38	40	42]	in.
81	[86	91	97	102	107]	cm

YARN

Rowan *Kidsilk Haze* in Majestic 589 (see page 118 for yarn information)

3	[4	4	4	4	4]	balls

NEEDLES

1 pair size 3 (3¼mm) needles
1 pair size 5 (3¾mm) needles

BUTTONS

3 x etched brass buttons, ½ in. (15mm) in diameter

GAUGE

20 sts and 30 rows to 4 in. (10cm) measured over patt using size 5 (3¾mm) needles, *or size to obtain correct gauge.*

BACK

Using size 3 (3¼mm) needles cast on 145 [151: 157: 169: 175: 187] sts.
Row 1 (RS) K1, *yo, K5, lift 2nd, 3rd, 4th, and 5th sts on right needle over first st and off right needle, yo, K1, rep from * to end.
97 [101: 105: 113: 117: 125] sts.
Work in garter st for 3 rows, dec 0 [0: 0: 1: 0: 1] st at each end of last row and ending with RS facing for next row. 97 [101: 105: 111: 117: 123] sts.
Change to size 5 (3¾mm) needles.
Beg with a K row, work in St st as folls:
Work 14 rows, ending with RS facing for next row.
Next row (dec) (RS) K3, K2tog, K to last 5 sts, skp, K3.
Work 13 rows.
Rep last 14 rows 3 times more, then first of these rows (the dec row) again.
87 [91: 95: 101: 107: 113] sts.
Work even until back meas 11 [11: 10¾: 12: 11½: 12¼] in. (28 [28: 27: 30: 29: 31]cm), ending with RS facing for next row.
Work in garter st for 6 rows, ending with RS facing for next row.
Now work in **lace patt** as folls:
Row 1 (RS) K2 [1: 0: 3: 0: 3], (yo, skp, K1) 0 [1: 0: 0: 0: 0] times, *K2tog, yo, K1, yo, skp, K1, rep from * to last 1 [3: 5: 2: 5: 2] sts, (K2tog, yo) 0 [1: 1: 0: 1: 0] times, K1 [1: 1: 2: 1: 2], (yo, skp) 0 [0: 1: 0: 1: 0] times.
Row 2 Purl.
Row 3 K1 [2: 4: 1: 4: 1], (K2tog, yo, K3) 1 [0: 0: 0: 0: 0] times, *yo, sl 1, K2tog, psso, yo, K3, rep from * to last 3 [5: 1: 4: 1: 4] sts, (yo, sl 1, K2tog, psso, yo) 0 [1: 0: 1: 0: 1] times, (yo, skp) 1 [0: 0: 0: 0: 0] times, K1 [2: 1: 1: 1: 1].
Row 4 Purl.
These 4 rows form lace patt.
Cont in lace patt until back meas 13 [13: 12½: 13¾: 13½: 14¼] in. (33 [33: 32: 35: 34: 36]cm), ending with RS facing for next row.

Shape armholes

Keeping patt correct, bind off 3 [4: 4: 5: 5: 6] sts at beg of next 2 rows. 81 [83: 87: 91: 97: 101] sts.
Dec 1 st at each end of next 3 [3: 5: 5: 7: 7] rows, then on foll 4 [4: 3: 4: 3: 4] alt rows.
67 [69: 71: 73: 77: 79] sts.
Work even until armhole meas 7½ [7½: 8: 8: 8¼: 8¼] in. (19 [19: 20: 20: 21: 21]cm), ending with RS facing for next row.

Shape shoulders and back neck

Bind off 4 [5: 5: 5: 6: 6] sts at beg of next 2 rows.
59 [59: 61: 63: 65: 67] sts.
Next row (RS) Bind off 4 [5: 5: 5: 6: 6] sts, patt until there are 9 [8: 9: 10: 9: 10] sts on right needle and turn, leaving rem sts on a holder.
Work each side of neck separately.
Bind off 4 sts at beg of next row.
Bind off rem 5 [4: 5: 6: 5: 6] sts.
With RS facing, rejoin yarn to rem sts, bind off center 33 [33: 33: 33: 35: 35] sts, patt to end.
Complete to match first side, reversing shapings.

LEFT FRONT

Using size 3 (3¼mm) needles cast on 73 [73: 79: 85: 85: 91] sts.
Row 1 (RS) K1, *yo, K5, lift 2nd, 3rd, 4th, and 5th sts on right needle over first st and off right needle, yo, K1, rep from * to end. 49 [49: 53: 57: 57: 61] sts.
Work in garter st for 3 rows, dec 2 [0: 2: 3: 0: 1] sts evenly across last row and ending with RS facing for next row. 47 [49: 51: 54: 57: 60] sts.
Change to size 5 (3¾mm) needles.
Beg with a K row, work in St st as folls:
Work 14 rows, ending with RS facing for next row.**
Next row (dec) (RS) K3, K2tog, K to end.
Work 13 rows.
Rep last 14 rows 3 times more, then first of these rows (the dec row) again.
42 [44: 46: 49: 52: 55] sts.
Work even until left front meas 11 [11: 10½: 12: 11½: 12¼] in. (28 [28: 27: 30: 29: 31]cm), ending with RS facing for next row.
Work in garter st for 6 rows, ending with RS facing for next row.

Now work in lace patt as folls:
Row 1 (RS) K2 [1: 0: 3: 0: 3], (yo, skp, K1) 0 [1: 0: 0: 0: 0] times, *K2tog, yo, K1, yo, skp, K1, rep from * to last 4 sts, K2tog, yo, K2.
Row 2 Purl.
Row 3 K1 [2: 4: 1: 4: 1], (K2tog, yo, K3) 1 [0: 0: 0: 0: 0] times, *yo, sl 1, K2tog, psso, yo, K3, rep from * to end.
Row 4 Purl.
These 4 rows form lace patt.
Cont in lace patt until left front matches back to beg of armhole shaping, ending with RS facing for next row.

Shape armhole

Keeping patt correct, bind off 3 [4: 4: 5: 5: 6] sts at beg of next row. 39 [40: 42: 44: 47: 49] sts.
Work 1 row.
Dec 1 st at armhole edge of next 3 [3: 5: 5: 7: 7] rows, then on foll 4 [4: 3: 4: 3: 4] alt rows.
32 [33: 34: 35: 37: 38] sts.
Work even until armhole meas 2½ [2½: 2¾: 2½: 2¾: 2¾] in. (6 [6: 7: 6: 7: 7]cm), ending with WS facing for next row.

Shape neck

Keeping patt correct, bind off 6 [6: 6: 6: 7: 7] sts at beg of next row. 26 [27: 28: 29: 30: 31] sts.
Dec 1 st at neck edge of next 7 rows, then on foll 5 alt rows, then on foll 4th row.
13 [14: 15: 16: 17: 18] sts.
Work even until left front matches back to beg of shoulder shaping, ending with RS facing for next row.

Shape shoulder

Bind off 4 [5: 5: 5: 6: 6] sts at beg of next and foll alt row.
Work 1 row.
Bind off rem 5 [4: 5: 6: 5: 6] sts.

RIGHT FRONT

Work as given for left front to **.
Next row (dec) (RS) K to last 5 sts, skp, K3.
Work 13 rows.
Rep last 14 rows 3 times more, then first of these rows (the dec row) again. 42 [44: 46: 49: 52: 55] sts.
Work even until right front meas 11 [11: 10¾: 12:

11½: 12¼] in. (28 [28: 27: 30: 29: 31]cm), ending with RS facing for next row.

Work in garter st for 6 rows, ending with RS facing for next row.

Now work in lace patt as folls:

Row 1 (RS) K2, yo, skp, K1, *K2tog, yo, K1, yo, skp, K1, rep from * to last 1 [3: 5: 2: 5: 2] sts, (K2tog, yo) 0 [1: 1: 0: 1: 0] times, K1 [1: 1: 2: 1: 2], (yo, skp) 0 [0: 1: 0: 1: 0] times.

Row 2 Purl.

Row 3 K3, *yo, sl 1, K2tog, psso, yo, K3, rep from * to last 3 [5: 1: 4: 1: 4] sts, (yo, sl 1, K2tog, psso, yo) 0 [1: 0: 1: 0: 1] times, (yo, skp) 1 [0: 0: 0: 0: 0] times, K1 [2: 1: 1: 1: 1].

Row 4 Purl.

These 4 rows form lace patt.

Complete to match left front, reversing shapings.

UNDER SLEEVES

Using size 3 (3¼mm) needles cast on 109 [109: 115: 115: 121: 121] sts.

Row 1 (RS) K1, *yo, K5, lift 2nd, 3rd, 4th, and 5th sts on right needle over first st and off right needle, yo, K1, rep from * to end.

73 [73: 77: 77: 81: 81] sts.

Row 2 (P2tog) 1 [0: 1: 0: 1: 0] times, P to last 2 [0: 2: 0: 2: 0] sts, (P2tog) 1 [0: 1: 0: 1: 0] times.

71 [73: 75: 77: 79: 81] sts.

Change to size 5 (3¾mm) needles.

Now work in lace patt as folls:

Row 1 (RS) K0 [1: 2: 3: 1: 2], (yo, skp, K1) 0 [0: 0: 0: 1: 1] times, *K2tog, yo, K1, yo, skp, K1, rep from * to last 5 [0: 1: 2: 3: 4] sts, (K2tog, yo) 1 [0: 0: 0: 1: 1] times, K1 [0: 1: 2: 1: 2], (yo, skp) 1 [0: 0: 0: 0: 0] times.

Row 2 Purl.

Row 3 K4 [0: 1: 1: 2: 3], (K2tog, yo, K3) 0 [1: 1: 0: 0: 0] times, *yo, sl 1, K2tog, psso, yo, K3, rep from * to last 1 [2: 3: 4: 5: 0] sts, (yo, sl 1, K2tog, psso, yo) 0 [0: 0: 1: 1: 0] times, (yo, skp) 0 [1: 1: 0: 0: 0] times, K1 [0: 1: 1: 2: 0].

Row 4 Purl.

These 4 rows form lace patt.

Cont in patt until sleeve meas 2 in. (5cm), ending

with RS facing for next row.

Shape top

Keeping patt correct, bind off 3 [4: 4: 5: 5: 6] sts at beg of next 2 rows. 65 [65: 67: 67: 69: 69] sts.

Dec 1 st at each end of next 5 rows, then on every foll alt row until 35 sts rem, then on foll 9 rows, ending with RS facing for next row.

Bind off rem 17 sts.

OVER SLEEVES

Using size 3 (3¼mm) needles cast on 115 [121: 121: 127: 127: 133] sts.

Row 1 (RS) K1, *yo, K5, lift 2nd, 3rd, 4th, and 5th sts on right needle over first st and off right needle, yo, K1, rep from * to end.

77 [81: 81: 85: 85: 89] sts.

Row 2 (P2tog) 0 [1: 0: 1: 0: 1] times, P to last 0 [2: 0: 2: 0: 2] sts, (P2tog) 0 [1: 0: 1: 0: 1] times.

77 [79: 81: 83: 85: 87] sts.

Change to size 5 (3¾mm) needles.

Now work in lace patt as given for under sleeves until sleeve meas ¾ in. (2cm), ending with RS facing for next row.

Shape top

Keeping patt correct, bind off 3 [4: 4: 5: 5: 6] sts at beg of next 2 rows. 1 [71: 73: 73: 75: 75] sts.

Dec 1 st at each end of next 11 rows, then on every foll alt row until 35 sts rem, then on foll 9 rows, ending with RS facing for next row.

Bind off rem 17 sts.

FINISHING

Press as described on the information page (see page 116).

Join both shoulder seams using back stitch, or mattress stitch if preferred.

Neckband

With RS facing and using size 3 (3¼mm) needles, beg and ending at front opening edges, pick up and knit 36 [36: 36: 38: 39: 39] sts up right side of neck, 41 [41: 41: 41: 43: 43] sts from back, then 36 [36: 36: 38: 39: 39] sts down left side of neck. 113 [113: 113: 117: 121: 121] sts.

Work in garter st for 6 rows, ending with WS facing

for next row.

Bind off knitwise (on WS).

Button band

With RS facing and using size 3 (3¼mm) needles, beg at bound-off edge of neckband, pick up and knit 81 [81: 81: 85: 85: 89] sts evenly down entire left front opening edge to cast-on edge.

Work in garter st for 6 rows, ending with WS facing for next row.

Bind off knitwise (on WS).

Buttonhole band

With RS facing and using size 3 (3¼mm) needles, beg at cast-on edge, pick up and knit 81 [81: 81: 85: 85: 89] sts evenly up entire right front opening edge to bound-off edge of neckband.

Work in garter st for 3 rows, ending with RS facing for next row.

Row 4 (RS) K to last 23 sts, (yo, K2tog, K8) twice, yo, K2tog, K1.

Work in garter st for a further 2 rows, ending with WS facing for next row.

Binf off knitwise (on WS).

Lay WS of over sleeves against RS of under sleeves and sew together around sleeve top. See information page for finishing instructions, setting in sleeves using the set-in method.

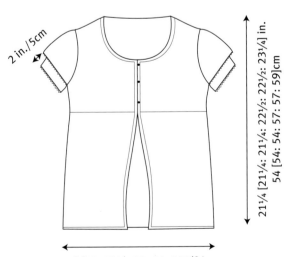

2 in./5cm

21¼ [21¼: 21¼: 22½: 22½: 23¼] in.
54 [54: 54: 57: 57: 59]cm

17¼ [18: 18¾: 20: 21: 22¼] in.
43.5 [45.5: 47.5: 50.5: 53.5: 56.5]cm

useful information

GAUGE

Obtaining the correct gauge is perhaps the single factor which can make the difference between a successful garment and a disastrous one. It controls both the shape and size of an article, so any variation, however slight, can distort the finished garment. We recommend that you knit a square in pattern and/or stockinette stitch (depending on the pattern instructions) with perhaps 5–10 more stitches and 5–10 more rows than those given in the gauge note. Mark out the central 4 in. (10cm) square with pins. If you have too many stitches to 4 in. (10cm), try again using thicker needles; if you have too few stitches to 4 in. (10cm), try again using finer needles. Once you have achieved the correct gauge your garment will be knitted to the measurements indicated in the schematic shown at the end of the pattern.

SIZING AND SCHEMATIC NOTE

The instructions are given for the smallest size. Where they vary, work the figures in brackets for the larger sizes. One set of figures refers to all sizes. Included with most patterns in this book is a "schematic" or sketch of the finished garment and its dimensions. The schematic shows the finished width of the garment at the underarm point, and it is this measurement that the knitter should go by when working out the right size; a useful tip is to measure one of your own garments which is a comfortable fit. Having chosen a size based on width, look at the corresponding length for that size; if you are not happy with the total length which we recommend, adjust your own garment before beginning your armhole shaping—any adjustment after this point will mean that your sleeve will not fit into your garment easily—don't forget to take your adjustment into account if there is any side seam shaping. Finally, look at the sleeve length; the schematic shows the finished sleeve measurement, taking into account any top-arm insertion length. Measure your body between the center of your neck and your wrist, this measurement should correspond to half the garment width plus the sleeve length. Again, your sleeve length may be adjusted, but remember to take into consideration your sleeve increases if you do adjust the length—you must increase more frequently than the pattern states to shorten your sleeve, less frequently to lengthen it.

FINISHING INSTRUCTIONS

It can take many hours to knit a garment, so it is a shame that many garments are spoiled because such little care is taken in the pressing and finishing process. The following tips offer a truly professional-looking garment.

PRESSING

Pin out each piece of knitting on a board (known as blocking) and, following the instructions on the yarn label, press the garment pieces, omitting the ribs. (NOTE: Take special care to press the edges, as this will make sewing up both easier and neater.) If the yarn label indicates that the fabric is not to be pressed, then covering the blocked-out fabric with a damp white cotton cloth and leaving it to stand will have the desired effect. Darn in all ends neatly along the selvage edge or a color join, as appropriate.

STITCHING

When stitching the pieces together, remember to match areas of color and texture very carefully where they meet. Use back stitch or mattress stitch for all main knitting seams and join all ribs and neckband with mattress stitch, unless otherwise stated.

CONSTRUCTION

Having completed the pattern instructions, join left shoulder and neckband seams as detailed above. Sew the top of the sleeve to the body of the garment using the method detailed in the pattern, referring to the appropriate guide:

Shallow set-in sleeves: Match decreases at beginning of armhole shaping to decreases at top of sleeve. Sew sleeve head into armhole, easing in shapings.

Set-in sleeves: Place center of bound-off edge of sleeve to shoulder seam. Set in sleeve, easing sleeve head into armhole.

Join side and sleeve seams.

Slip stitch pocket edgings and linings into place.

Sew on buttons to correspond with buttonholes.

Ribbed welts and neckbands and any areas of garter stitch should not be pressed.

SIZE GUIDE

The sizing conforms to standard clothing sizes. Therefore if you buy a standard US size 10 in clothing, then the size 10 (or Medium) patterns in this book will fit you perfectly.

Dimensions in the chart (right) are body measurements, not garment dimensions, therefore please refer to the measuring guide to help you to determine which is the best size for you to knit.

MEASURING GUIDE

For maximum comfort and to ensure the correct fit when choosing a size to knit, please follow the tips below when checking your size.

Measure yourself close to your body, over your underwear, and don't pull the tape measure too tight!

Bust/chest—measure around the fullest part of the bust/chest and across the shoulder blades.

Waist—measure around the natural waistline, just above the hip bone.

Hips—measure around the fullest part of the bottom.

If you don't wish to measure yourself, note the size of a favorite sweater that you like the fit of. Measure your favorite sweater and then compare these

STANDARD SIZING GUIDE FOR WOMEN

UK Size	8	10	12	14	16	18	20	22	
USA Size	6	8	10	12	14	16	18	20	
EUR Size	34	36	38	40	42	44	46	48	
To fit bust	32	34	36	38	40	42	44	46	in.
	82	87	92	97	102	107	112	117	cm
To fit waist	24	26	28	30	32	34	36	38	in.
	61	66	71	76	81	86	91	96	cm
To fit hips	34	6	38	40	42	44	46	48	in.
	87	92	97	102	107	112	117	122	cm

measurements with the schematic given at the end of the individual instructions.

SPECIAL NOTE: Remember if your gauge is too loose, your garment will be bigger than the pattern size and you may use more yarn. If your gauge is too tight, your garment could be smaller than the pattern size and you will have yarn left over. Furthermore if your gauge is incorrect, the handle of your fabric will be too stiff or floppy and will not fit properly. It really does make sense to check your gauge before starting every project.

ABBREVIATIONS

alt	alternate	M1	make one stitch by picking up horizontal loop before next stitch and knitting back of it	rep	repeat
beg	begin(ning)			RS	right side
cont	continue			rev St st	reverse stockinette stitch (1 row P, 1 row K)
cm	centimeters				
dec	decreas(e)(ing)	mm	millimeters	skp	(slip 1, knit 1, psso)
foll	following	patt	pattern	sl1	slip one stitch
in.(s)	inch(es)	P	purl	st(s)	stitch(es)
inc	increas(e)(ing)	P2tog	purl next 2 stitches together	St st	stockinette stitch (1 row K, 1 row P)
K	knit				
K2tog	knit next 2 stitches together	psso	pass slipped stitch over no stitches, times, or rows for that size	tbl	through back of loop(s)
				tog	together
meas	measures			WS	wrong side
		rem	remain(ing)	yo	yarn over needle

yarn information

The following yarns are those specified in the patterns in this book. Rowan *Felted Tweed*, *Felted Tweed Aran*, and *Felted Tweed Chunky* have replaced Rowan *Tweed Scottish Tweed DK*, *Aran*, and *Chunky* used in some of the original patterns. Rowan *Cashsoft 4-ply* replaces Rowan *4-ply soft* used in one original pattern. When using substitute yarns, always take care to check your gauge carefully by knitting a preliminary gauge square and by altering knitting needle sizes as necessary to obtain the specified gauge in the pattern. Failure to obtain the correct gauge will affect the fit/size of the relevant garment.

Rowan *All Seasons Cotton* 4 Medium

A worsted weight cotton-acrylic/microfiber mix yarn; 60 percent cotton, 40 percent acrylic/microfiber; 1³⁄₄oz/50g (approximately 98yd/90m) per ball. Recommended gauge: 16–18sts and 23–25 rows to 4in./10cm measured over St st using sizes 7–9 (4.5–5.5mm) knitting needles.

Rowan *Calmer* 3 Light

A lightweight cotton-acrylic microfiber mix yarn; 75 percent cotton; 25 percent acrylic microfiber; 1³⁄₄oz/50g (approximately 175yd/160m) per ball. Recommended gauge: 21sts and 30 rows to 4in./10cm measured over St st using size 8 (5mm) knitting needles.

Rowan *Classic Cashsoft 4-ply* 1 Super Fine
(to replace Rowan *4-ply soft*)

A superfine-weight wool-and-cashmere mix yarn; 57 percent fine merino wool, 33 percent microfiber, 10 percent cashmere; 1³⁄₄oz/50g (approximately 197yd/180m) per ball. Recommended gauge: 28sts and 36 rows to 4in./10cm measured over St st using size 3 (3¼mm) knitting needles.

Rowan *Felted Tweed* 3 Light
(to replace Rowan *Scottish Tweed DK*)

A lightweight wool-alpaca-viscose mix; 50 percent merino wool, 25 percent alpaca wool, 25 percent viscose; 1³⁄₄oz/50g (approximately 191yd/175m) per ball. Recommended gauge: 22–24 sts and 30–32 rows to 4in./10cm measured over St st using sizes 5–6 (3¼–4mm) knitting needles.

Rowan *Felted Tweed Aran* 4 Medium
(to replace Rowan *Scottish Tweed Aran*)

An Aran weight merino wool-alpaca-viscose mix yarn; 50 percent merino wool, 25 percent alpaca, 15 percent viscose. 1³⁄₄oz/50g (95yd/87m) per ball. Recommended gauge: 16sts and 23 rows to 4in./10cm measured over St st using size 8 (5mm) knitting needles.

Rowan *Felted Tweed Chunky* 6 Super Bulky
(to replace Rowan *Scottish Tweed Chunky*)

A bulky merino wool-alpaca-viscose mix yarn; 50 percent merino wool, 25 percent alpaca, 15 percent viscose; 1³⁄₄oz/50g (55yd/50m) per ball. Recommended gauge: 11sts and 14 rows to 4in./10cm measured over St st using size 11 (8mm) knitting needles.

Rowan *Kidsilk Aura* 4 Medium

A worsted/Aran weight mohair-silk mix yarn, 75 percent kid mohair, 25 percent silk; ⁷⁄₈oz/25g (approximately 82yd/75m) per ball. Recommended gauge: 16–20 sts and 19–28 rows to 4in./10cm measured over St st using sizes 6–10 (4–6mm) knitting needles.

Rowan *Kid Classic* 4 Medium

A worsted weight lambswool-mohair-nylon mix yarn, 70 percent lambswool, 25 percent kid mohair, 4 percent nylon; 1³⁄₄oz/50g (153yd/140m) per ball. Recommended gauge: 18–19 sts and 23–25 rows to 4in./10cm measured over St st using sizes 8–9 (5–5½ mm) knitting needles.

Rowan *Kidsilk Haze* 2 Fine

A fine-weight mohair mix yarn; 70 percent super kid mohair, 30 percent silk; ⁷⁄₈oz/25g (approximately 229yd/210m) per ball. Recommended gauge: 18–25 sts and 23–34 rows to 4in./10cm measured over St st using sizes 3–8 (3¼–5mm) knitting needles.

Rowan *Wool Cotton* 3 Light

A lightweight wool/cotton blend yarn; 50 percent merino wool, 50 percent cotton; 1³⁄₄oz/50g (approximately 123yd/113m) per ball; recommended gauge: 22–24sts and 30–32 rows to 4in./10cm measured over St st using sizes 5–6 (3¼–4mm) knitting needles.

buying yarns

Rowan yarns (and buttons) have been used for all the knitting patterns in this book. See opposite for descriptions of the yarns used. To find out where to buy Rowan yarns near you, contact one of the Rowan yarn distributors given below. The main Rowan office is in the United Kingdom (see below for their website).

ROWAN YARN DISTRIBUTORS

U.S.A.
Westminster Fibers Inc,
165 Ledge Street, Nashua,
New Hampshire 03060
Tel: 1-800-445-9276
www.westminsterfibers.com

U.K.
Rowan, Green Lane Mill, Holmfirth,
West Yorkshire, HD9 2DX
Tel: +44 (0) 1484 681881
Fax: +44 (0) 1484 687920
Email: mail@knitrowan.com
www.knitrowan.com

AUSTRALIA
Australian Country Spinners,
Pty Ltd,
Level 7, 409 St. Kilda Road,
Melbourne Vic 3004
Tel: 03 9380 3830
Fax: 03 9820 0989
Email: sales@auspinners.com.au

AUSTRIA
Coats Harlander GmbH,
Autokaderstrasse 31,
A-1210 Wien.
Tel: (01) 27716 - 0
Fax: (01) 27716 - 228

BELGIUM
Coats Benelux, Ring Oost 14A,
Ninove, 9400, Belgium
Tel: 0346 35 37 00
Email:
sales.coatsninove@coats.com

CANADA
Westminster Fibers Inc,
165 Ledge Street, Nashua,
New Hampshire 03060
Tel: 1-800-445-9276
www.westminsterfibers.com

CHINA
Coats Shanghai Ltd, No 9 Building,
Baosheng Road,
Songjiang Industrial Zone,
Shanghai.
Tel: (86-21) 5774 3733
Fax: (86-21) 5774 3768

DENMARK
Coats Danmark A/S,
Nannasgade 28,
2200 Kobenhavn N
Tel: (45) 35 86 90 50
Fax: (45) 35 82 15 10
Email: info@hpgruppen.dk
www.hpgruppen.dk

FINLAND
Coats Opti Oy, Ketjutie 3,
04220 Kerava
Tel: (358) 9 274 871
Fax: (358) 9 2748 7330
Email: coatsopti.sales@coats.com

FRANCE
Coats France / Steiner Frères,
SAS 100, avenue du Général de Gaulle,
18 500 Mehun-Sur-Yèvre
Tel: (33) 02 48 23 12 30
Fax: (33) 02 48 23 12 40

GERMANY
Coats GmbH, Kaiserstrasse 1,
D-79341 Kenzingen
Tel: (49) 7644 8020
Fax: (49) 7644 802399
www.coatsgmbh.de

HOLLAND
Coats Benelux, Ring Oost 14A,
Ninove, 9400, Belgium
Tel: 0346 35 37 00
Email:
sales.coatsninove@coats.com

HONG KONG
Coats China Holdings Ltd,
19/F Millennium City 2,
378 Kwun Tong Road,
Kwun Tong, Kowloon
Tel: (852) 2798 6886
Fax: (852) 2305 0311

ICELAND
Storkurinn, Laugavegi 59,
101 Reykjavik
Tel: (354) 551 8258
Email: storkurinn@simnet.is

ITALY
Coats Cucirini s.r.l., Via Sarca 223,
20126 Milano
Tel: 800 992377
Fax: 0266111701
Email: servizio.clienti@coats.com

KOREA
Coats Korea Co Ltd, 5F Kuckdong
B/D, 935-40 Bangbae-Dong,
Seocho-Gu, Seoul
Tel: (82) 2 521 6262.
Fax: (82) 2 521 5181

LEBANON
y.knot, Saifi Village,
Mkhalissiya Street 162, Beirut
Tel: (961) 1 992211
Fax: (961) 1 315553
Email: y.knot@cyberia.net.lb

LUXEMBOURG
Coats Benelux, Ring Oost 14A,
Ninove, 9400, Belgium
Tel: 054 318989
Email:
sales.coatsninove@coats.com

MALTA
John Gregory Ltd, 8 Ta'Xbiex Sea
Front, Msida MSD 1512.
Tel: (356) 2133 0202
Fax: (356) 2134 4745,
Email: raygreg@onvol.net

MEXICO
Estambres Crochet SA de CV,
Aaron Saenz
1891-7, Monterrey, NL 64650.
Tel: +52 (81) 8335-3870

NEW ZEALAND
ACS New Zealand, 1 March Place,
Belfast, Christchurch
Tel: 64-3-323-6665
Fax: 64-3-323-6660

NORWAY
Coats Knappehuset AS,
Pb 100 Ulset, 5873 Bergen
Tel: (47) 55 53 93 00
Fax: (47) 55 53 93 93

SINGAPORE
Golden Dragon Store,
101 Upper Cross Street #02-51,
People's Park Centre,
Singapore 058357
Tel: (65) 6 5358454
Fax: (65) 6 2216278
Email: gdscraft@hotmail.com

SOUTH AFRICA
Arthur Bales LTD, 62 4th Avenue,
Linden 2195
Tel: (27) 11 888 2401
Fax: (27) 11 782 6137
Email: arthurb@new.co.za

SPAIN
Coats Fabra, Santa Adria 20,
08030 Barcelona
Tel: 932908400
Fax: 932908409
Email: tencion.clientes@coats.com

SWEDEN
Coats Expotex AB, Division Craft,
Box 297, 401 24 Goteborg
Tel: (46) 33 720 79 00
Fax: (46) 31 47 16 50

SWITZERLAND
Coats Stroppel AG, Stroppelstr.16
CH-5300 Turgi (AG)
Tel: (41) 562981220
Fax: (41) 56 298 12 50

TAIWAN
Cactus Quality Co Ltd, P.O.Box 30
485, Taipei, Taiwan, R.O.C., Office:
7FL-2, No 140, Roosevelt Road,
Sec 2,Taipei, Taiwan, R.O.C.
Tel: 886-2-23656527
Fax: 886-2-23656503
Email: cqcl@m17.hinet.net

THAILAND
Global Wide Trading,
10 Lad Prao Soi 88,
Bangkok 10310
Tel: 00 662 933 9019
Fax: 00 662 933 9110
Email: global.wide@yahoo.com

acknowledgments

We would like to thank the following for their help in producing the original brochures from which this edition has been compiled:
For design layout: brochure 2, 3, 5 Lee Wills; brochure 8: Graham McWilliam and Lisa Richardson; brochure 12, Lisa Richardson. For hair and make up: brochures 2 and 3: Jonothan Malone; brochures 5, 8, and 12: Jeni Dodson. Models: brochures 2, 3, and 8: Martha at M & P Model Management; brochure 5: Lucy Nontha at Models 1; brochure 12: Emily Byron at Select Models. For styling: brochure 2: Jo Barker; brochure 2, 3, 5, and 12: Sarah Hatton.

Rowan would also like to thank Sue Whiting for her help in providing updated yarns for the patterns in this edition.